God's Marvelous Book—The Bible

By David C. Bennett, D. Min.

Published by

THE BIBLE FOR TODAY PRESS

900 Park Avenue

Collingswood, New Jersey 08108

U.S.A.

Church Phone: 856-854-4747

BFT Phone: 856-854-4452

Orders: 1-800-John 10:9

e-mail: BFT@BibleForToday.org

Website: www.BibleForToday.org

fax: 856-854-2464

We Use and Defend

the King James Bible

February, 2013

BFT #4050

ISBN #978-1-56848-083-1

Table Of Contents

Preface

I appreciate my pastor, Dr. D. A. Waite, who is knowledgeable in Biblical Greek and has been a BIG help in getting this book into print. He truly is a scholar whom one can trust when it comes to this issue of the Greek Text and the English Bible.

When the Lord opened my understanding to this issue of the Greek Text and English Bibles, I began writing various papers in defense of the Greek text underlying our King James Bible. In writing those papers, I heard back from some who were in disagreement and others who were in agreement.

This small book is for both those groups. It is not a "scholarly" book, but my prayer is perhaps it will be used of the Lord to help some who once disagreed to change and to encourage even more the ones who agreed.

For the Words of God,

David C. Bennett

David C. Bennett, D. Min.

ꜰoreword

- **The Need**. There is a great need for those of us who stand together on the principles of the King James Bible and its underlying Hebrew, Aramaic, and Greek Words to do research, and then, speak and write about the needed defense of these truths. By the writing of this book, Dr. Bennett has helped to answer this need.

- **The Author.** Dr. David Bennett is the author of this book. He has been one of the missionaries of the **Bible ꜰor Today Baptist Church** for many years. Our church is his "sending church." He and his wife, Pam, have been serving the Lord Jesus Christ in the land of Australia. He has a church and a radio ministry there.   He is also one of our faithful Executive Committee members of the Dean Burgon Society (DBS).

- **The Book's Format.** I have taken Dr. Bennett's book and put it into a format that could be used for the printing of the book. Though this has taken some time and patience, it was necessary to be done before it could be sent to the publishers.

- **The Book's Usefulness.** It is our hope and prayer that this book might be used of the Lord to convince and encourage even further those who stand with us on the King James Bible and its underlying original Words. It is also our hope that it might convert to the Bible's truth, those who have been blinded by the modern versions and their corrupted original words.

- **The Readers.** It is hoped that those who receive and read this book might encourage many others to get the book, read it and urge others to read it as well.

Yours For God's Words,

D. A. Waite

Pastor D. A. Waite, Th.D., Ph.D.

Bible ꜰor Today Baptist Church

𝔄cknowledgments

The 𝔅ible 𝔉or 𝔗oday 𝔅aptist 𝔠hurch wishes to thank and to acknowledge the assistance of the following people:

- **The Congregation** of the 𝔅ible 𝔉or 𝔗oday 𝔅aptist 𝔠hurch who received copies of the book and paid for its publication.

- **Pam Bennett**--Dr. Bennett's wife, who read the manuscript and suggested various items for consideration.

- **Yvonne Sanborn Waite**--Pastor Waite's wife, who read the manuscript, and gave helpful suggestions and comments.

- **Julie Monaghan**--who volunteered to help with the proofreading of the book, she had many suggestions for commas for clarity, as well as other helpful changes.

- **Anne Marie Noyle**--a faithful church supporter and Internet attender from Canada who proofread the book and gave many useful suggestions for improvement and clarification.

CHAPTER ONE

IS THE KING JAMES BIBLE INSPIRED?

2 Timothy 3:16 *"All scripture is given by inspiration (θεόπνευστος) of God, and is profitable for doctrine, for reproof, for correction, for instruction in righteousness".*

As a missionary, I have attended and preached in a lot of Baptist churches which hold different views on diverse theological subjects. For instance, some churches hold to a stricter ecclesiastical separation than others do. Some use the King James Bible without any particular belief as to why, while others use the King James because they believe it is the best English translation based on the original preserved Words.

In this book the following will be considered:

The first subject considered in this paper is that of the INSPIRATION of the Scriptures. The word inspiration (theopneustos) is used only in this one text, 2 Timothy 3:16, in the whole of Scripture. Strong's on-line Concordance gives the following;

"theopneustos: God-breathed, i.e. inspired by God

Original Word: θεόπνευστος, ον
Part of Speech: Adjective
Transliteration: theopneustos
Phonetic Spelling: (theh-op'-nyoo-stos)
Short Definition: God-breathed, inspired by God
Definition: God-breathed, inspired by God, due to the inspiration of God."[1]

Strong's on-line Exhaustive Concordance states:

"given by inspiration of God."

From theos and a presumed derivative of pneo; divinely breathed in-- given by inspiration of God."[2]

The Bible is a unique Book and a believer cannot approach the Bible like any other book. Dr. Jack Moorman wrote:

> "*Three kinds of books have been written on this subject. The first is from a totally naturalistic viewpoint, with the author denying that there was anything supernatural about the Bible's production and transmission. The second affirms the Bible's inspiration but takes a basically naturalistic position regarding its transmission.*"[3]

Brother Moorman continues by stating that:

> "*It is not really possible to be neutral about the Bible. If you try to be neutral, if you ignore the divine inspiration and the providential preservation of the Bible and treat it like an ordinary human book, then you are ignoring the very factors that make the Bible what it is.*"[4]

Dr. Floyd Nolan Jones in *WHICH VERSION* page five wrote that:

> "*Within our diverse denominational backgrounds are found various confessions of faith. These statements of*

---

[1] http://concordances.org/greek/2315.htm

[2] http://concordances.org/greek/2315.htm

[3] Jack Moorman, FOREVER SETTLED, pdf, page 1.

[4] Jack Moorman, FOREVER SETTLED, pdf, page 34.

faith concerning the Holy Scriptures, particularly within conservative evangelical backgrounds, always say something to the effect that we believe that God gave the original Scriptures inerrant. We profess to believe in the originals, that they were divinely inspired by God–God breathed."

Dr. Jones later states that:

"Today, most conservative Protestant clergymen have been brainwashed as mere youths in their late teens or early twenties at the various denominational Bible colleges and seminaries concerning the doctrine of inerrancy of Scripture. As a result, when most of these pastors etc., declare that they believe in the verbal, plenary inspiration and/or inerrancy (or some other similar declaration of faith in the Scriptures) what they really mean is that only the original autographa were inerrant."[5]

Dr. Jeffery Khoo in his booklet *KEPT PURE IN ALL AGES* writes on page 22 that:

"The words 'given by inspiration of God' in 2 Timothy 3:16 come from one Greek word theopneustos which literally means 'God breathed.' It is thus not 'manspiration,' but 'Godspiration.' God used human writers to pen His words. These men were specially chosen by God, and perfectly guided by the Spirit to put on paper the very words of God, and to do so without any error (2 Peter 1:21)."

Southern Baptist Basil Manly, Jr. believed:

"an uninspired Bible would 'furnish no infallible standard of truth,' and would leave us open to the mistakes and errors in judgment of the human authors.

---

[5] Floyd Nolan Jones, WHICH VERSION IS THE BIBLE?, KingsWord Press, Five Milan Hwy., Humboldt, TN 38343, p. 184

'It would furnish no principle of accurate discrimination between the true and false, the divine and the human.'"[6]

Manly believed in plenary (full, complete) inspiration and wrote:

"The doctrine which we hold is that commonly styled Plenary Inspiration or Full Inspiration. It is that the Bible as a whole is the Word of God, so that in every part of Scripture there is both infallible truth and divine authority."[7]

The Dean Burgon Society (DBS) of which I am a member, states:

*"As the Bible uses it, the term "inspiration" refers to the **writings**, not the **writers** (2 **Timothy** 3:16-17); the **writers** are spoken of as being "holy men of God" who were "moved," "carried" or "borne" along by the Holy Spirit (2 **Peter** 1:21) in such a definite way that their **writings** were supernaturally, plenarily, and verbally inspired, free from any error, infallible, and inerrant, as no other **writings** have ever been or ever will be inspired."[8]*

The Dean Burgon Society is named after Anglican John Burgon who wrote:

"The Bible is none other than the voice of Him that sitteth upon the throne. Every book of it, every chapter of it, every verse of it, every syllable of it, every letter of it, is direct utterance of the Most High. The Bible is none other than the Word of God, not some part of it more, some part of it less, but all alike the utterance of Him that sitteth upon the throne, faultless, unerring, supreme."[9]

---

[6] L. Russ Bush and Tom J. Nettles, BAPTISTS AND THE BIBLE, Moody Press, Chicago, 1980, page 212.

[7] Ibid.

[8] http://www.deanburgonsociety.org/DBS_Society/articles.htm

[9] Timothy Tow and Jeffrey Khoo, A THEOLOGY FOR EVERY CHRISTIAN, Far Eastern Bible College Press Singapore, 1998, pdf, page 19.

Therefore, it is agreed by Bible believing-Christians that the Bible, both Old and New Testaments are the very breathed-out Words of God and given to men who penned these Words down. The material upon which God breathed-out His Words are the original documents.

It is to be understood that conservative Baptists agree inspiration applies to the original autographs, but as Dr. Floyd Nolan Jones states:

> *"It may surprise many to learn that there are no original manuscripts of the Bible available today. The Old Testament scribes destroyed the scrolls upon which Scripture was written as they became worn, and 'dog-eared' from so much handling. When they copied out a new one, they destroyed the old so that the earliest Old Testament manuscript now in existence is dated about 900 A.D. This is called the Hebrew Masoretic Text. It was the earliest witness to the text of the O.T. that we possessed until the discovery of the Dead Sea Scrolls which contain some parts of the Old Testament, especially Isaiah. Likewise, we possess no 'original' New Testament manuscripts–none of the 'autographs' which the apostles wrote have been preserved."* [10]

Does this leave the churches in a dilemma?

The General Association of Regular Baptists in their Baptist Bulletin of June, 2011 says:

> *"none of these manuscripts exists today. The Greek and Hebrew manuscripts that we have are various copies produced by scribes through the ages."* [11]

So we had original documents with the breathed-out Words of God, but those documents are no longer available.

Because the writers of the original manuscripts only wrote once, these originals had to be copied and spread among the churches. These copies were copied and those copies were copied. As the copies were used over and over,

---

[10] Floyd Nolan Jones, WHICH VERSION IS THE BIBLE?, KingsWord Press, Five Milan Hwy., Humboldt, TN 38343, pp. 5, 6

[11] http://baptistbulletin.org/?p=16799

they too had to be copied. So did God, by His providence, preserve His Words via those copies produced from those original written God-breathed Words? Therefore, it is justifiable to ask the question, where are those Words today?

So here is a brief review. The original Old Testament manuscripts and the original New Testament manuscripts were God's breathed-out Words given to men who penned those exact Words via their own personality on "paper." However, those original documents containing the God-breathed-out Words were used and used until they were probably worn out through continuous use and are no longer available. But those documents containing those God-breathed Words were copied and recopied.

In 2 Timothy 3:16,

". . . *no reference is being made with regard to the 'ORIGINAL' Scriptures. Look at verse 15. Paul says to Timothy, 'from a child you have known the Holy Scriptures which are able to make you wise unto salvation.' Paul is obviously not speaking of the 'ORIGINAL' New Testament Scripture.*"

"*Second Timothy was penned about A.D. 65. Further, Timothy was old enough to join Paul and Silas c.53 A.D. (Acts 16:1–4). Thus, when Timothy was a child, there was no New Testament collection of Scripture anywhere. Nor was Paul speaking of the "ORIGINALS" of the Old Testament for there was not an original Old Testament piece of paper or vellum extant at that time. Wrestle with this! Come to grips with it! These are the verses upon which many of us base our faith and say we believe in the 'ORIGINALS'. Yet these very verses are not speaking of the original manuscripts!*"

"*But are the copies inspired? The Bible itself clearly teaches that faithful copies of the originals are also inspired. The word "Scripture" in 2 Timothy 3:16–17 is translated from the Greek word 'graphé' (γραφή). Graphé occurs 51 times in the Greek New Testament and at every occurrence it means "Scripture" –in fact, it usually refers to the Old Testament text.*"

"*A perusal of the N.T. reveals that the Lord Jesus read from the 'graphé' in the synagogue at Nazareth (Luke*

4:21) as did Paul in the synagogue at Thessalonica (Acts 17:2). The Ethiopian eunuch, returning home from worshipping at Jerusalem, was riding in his chariot and reading a passage of graphé (Acts 8:32–33). These were not the autographs that they were reading; they were copies – moreover, copies of copies! Yet the Word of God calls them graphé–and every graphé is "given by inspiration of God" (2 Timothy 3:16). Thus, the Holy Writ has testified and that testimony is that faithful copies of the originals are themselves inspired. Selah!"[12]

Now it MUST BE UNDERSTOOD AND EMPHASIZED that Dr. Jones is saying these copies were copies of the ORIGINAL WORDS written in Hebrew, some Aramaic, and Greek and were NOT TRANSLATIONS but copies of the ORIGINAL WORDS! INSPIRATION OF THOSE ORIGINAL WORDS ONLY OCCURRED ONCE! But accurate copies of those original God-breathed Words carry the same authority!

So where does that put the churches today? Do the churches have access to those original Words in any extant Greek copy? There are over five thousand manuscripts of the New Testament in existence today and the manuscript evidence supporting the Greek Text underlying the King James Bible is in the majority. It is that majority of manuscript evidence that is represented in Dr. Frederick H. A. Scrivener's Greek New Testament. The Dean Burgon Society says:

"We believe that Scrivener's Greek text which underlies our King James Bible is the closest to the original New Testament."[13]

It might interest some that:

"Dr. Scrivener chose to begin his task with Beza's 1598

---

[12] Floyd Nolan Jones, WHICH VERSION IS THE BIBLE?, KingsWord Press, Five Milan Hwy., Humboldt, TN 38343, pp. 7, 8

[13] Scrivener's Annotated Greek New Testament, Dean Burgon Society Press, Box 354, Collingswood, NJ, 08108, Dec., 1999, Publisher's Preface.

Greek edition. This slightly reduced the number of required changes (compared to starting with other Greek editions of Erasmus, Stephanus, Beza, or Elzevir). He also reasoned that 'between 1598 and 1611 no important edition appeared; so that Beza's fifth and last text of 1598 was more than likely than any other to be in the hands of the King James's revisers, and to be accepted by them as the best standard within their reach. Where the English of the KJV differed from Beza's 1598 Greek edition, Dr. Scrivener (in about 162 places) used readings from previous Greek editions of the Received Text. He kept Beza's 1598 readings in about 59 places where the KJV had only Latin support. He listed these c. 221 deviations from Beza's 1598 Greek edition in his 'Appendix' (pages 648–656)." [14]

So the churches do have a copy of those original Words, praise the Lord! However, as Dr. Floyd Jones has aptly written "*. . . it is not merely a question of 'inspiration'. The crux is that of **preservation**."* [15]

This subject of preservation will be discussed in Chapter Three. But, before we look at **PRESERVATION**, we will look at the **CORRUPTION** that occurred not long after the originals were written. As John Burgon wrote:

"Thus it appears that errors crept in at the very first commencement of the life of the Church. This is a matter so interesting and so important in the history of corruption, that I must venture to place it again before our readers." [16]

---

[14] D. A. Waite, Jr., The Doctored New Testament, The Bible For Today Press, 900 Park Av., Collingswood, NJ, 08108, p. viii.

[15] Floyd Nolan Jones, WHICH VERSION IS THE BIBLE?, KingsWord Press, Five Milan Hwy., Humboldt, TN 38343, page 1

[16] John William Burgon, THE CAUSES OF THE CORRUPTION OF THE TRADITIONAL TEXT OF THE HOLY GOSPELS, Christian Classics Ethereal Library, pdf. Page 12.

This CORRUPTION OF THE ORIGINAL WORDS OF GOD will be the subject of Chapter Two.

CHAPTER TWO

CORRUPTION OF THE NEW TESTAMENT MANUSCRIPTS

In the last Chapter, the subject before us was INSPIRATION. In Chapter Two, the subject will be the CORRUPTION of the New Testament. One of the meanings Webster's 1828 Dictionary gives for *"corrupt"* is *"To vitiate or deprave; to change from good to bad."*

That is exactly what took place almost as soon as the original New Testament writings were finished. As already noted in Chapter One, John William Burgon said:

> *"THUS IT APPEARS THAT ERRORS CREPT IN AT THE VERY FIRST COMMENCEMENT OF THE LIFE OF THE CHURCH. This is a matter so interesting and so important in the history of corruption, that I must venture to place it again before our readers."*[17]

Without question, the first corrupter of the Words of God was Satan. Satan began his corrupting the Words of God in the Garden of Eden when he stated to Eve, *"Yea, hath God said, Ye shall not eat of every tree of the garden?"*

---

[17] John William Burgon, THE CAUSES OF THE CORRUPTION OF THE TRADITIONAL TEXT OF THE HOLY GOSPELS, http://www.ccel.org/ccel/burgon/corruption.html, pdf. p.12.

Genesis 3: 1. That old serpent, the Devil, has been active in this enterprise ever since!

Satan's corrupting the Word of Life is also seen in Jehudi's taking a penknife to the Words that God had given Jeremiah. Without question, Jehudi's penknife procedure was the brain-child of Satan and this continues to be one of his favorites, performing the task through various individuals and groups.

This old Dragon has utilized various men down through the centuries to slash and cut the Words of the living God through the penknife procedure. This practice has brought us to the place where some men today aren't exactly certain where the Words of God are to be found but they are determined, however, to hopefully one day restore those original Words which God somehow allowed to be lost!

Edward Miller, an associate of Dean John William Burgon, agreed with the Dean when he wrote that:

> *"Very soon, therefore, after the books of the New Testament were written, corruption began to affect them."*[18]

Before going further into how the corrupters corrupted the Words of God it MUST be understood that:

> *". . . It can hardly be conceived that the Holy Ghost, after communicating His Inspiration in the composition of books, would in the midst of His overruling care have allowed those books to be varied according to changing winds of human opinion and human action, without the maintenance throughout of a form mainly at least free from error. It can scarcely be but that a succession of copies pure from any great corruption must have existed,*

---

[18] Edward Miller, A GUIDE TO THE TEXTUAL CRITICISM OF THE NEW TESTAMENT, pdf. p. 68.

and existed too in predominance, all down the Church's history."[19]

So, in spite of the corruption that many men intended to impose upon God's Words, the true Words continued to be used and copied.

Let it be known that those Original Words of God were never lost! However, with several Greek texts in existence today, it may be asked therefore:

"WHAT is the genuine Greek—what is the true Text of the New Testament? Which are the very words which were written by the Evangelists and Apostles of our Lord Jesus Christ under the Inspiration of the Holy Ghost?"[20]

The answer to this IMPORTANT question will become apparent in the Chapter on Preservation.

John Burgon's work *THE CAUSES OF THE CORRUPTION OF THE TRADITIONAL TEXT OF THE HOLY GOSPELS*[21] is a classic and invaluable source of information concerning this subject of the corruption of the New Testament. In this book, the Dean details in great length how these corruptions came to be in the Text of our New Testament. Brother Burgon states:

"The discussion on which I now enter is then on the Causes of the various Corruptions of the Text. The reader shall be shewn with illustrations to what particular source they are to be severally ascribed."[22]

He goes on to tell the reader that:

"When I take into my hands an ancient copy of the Gospels, I expect that it will exhibit sundry inaccuracies and imperfections: and I am never disappointed in my

---

[19] Edward Miller, A GUIDE TO THE TEXTUAL CRITICISM OF THE NEW TESTAMENT, pdf. p. 66.

[20] Ibid.,p. 1.

[21] http://www.ccel.org/ccel/burgon/corruption.toc.html

[22] Ibid. p.20

> *expectation. The discovery however creates no uneasiness, so long as the phenomena evolved are of a certain kind and range within easily definable limits."*[23]

Dean John Burgon knew what to look for so it is to this work we will quote from at length along with other books.

The Chapters in *THE CAUSES OF THE CORRUPTION OF THE TRADITIONAL TEST OF THE HOLY GOSPELS* are:

Chapter I. General Corruption.

Chapter II. Accidental Causes of Corruption. I. Pure Accident.

Chapter III. Accidental Causes of Corruption. II. Homoeoteleuton.

Chapter IV. Accidental Causes of Corruption. III. From Writing in Unicals.

Chapter V. Accidental Causes of Corruption. IV. Itacism.

Chapter VI. Accidental Causes of Corruption. V. Liturgical Influence.

Chapter VII. Causes of Corruption Chiefly Intentional. I. Harmonistic Influence.

Chapter VIII. Causes of Corruption Chiefly Intentional. II. Assimilation.

Chapter IX. Causes of Corruption Chiefly Intentional. III. Attraction.

Chapter X. Causes of Corruption Chiefly Intentional. IV. Omission.

Chapter XI. Causes of Corruption Chiefly Intentional. V. Transposition.

Chapter XI. Causes of Corruption Chiefly Intentional. VI. Substitution.

Chapter XI. (continued). Causes of Corruption Chiefly Intentional. VII. Addition.

Chapter XII. Causes of Corruption Chiefly Intentional. VIII. Glosses.

Chapter XIII. Causes of Corruption Chiefly Intentional. IX. Corruption by Heretics.

---

[23] Ibid. p. 20

Chapter XIV. Causes of Corruption Chiefly Intentional. X. Corruption by the Orthodox.[24]

It may be hard to understand that God allowed some corruption to occur inadvertently, but as Burgon writes:

> "*It may be regarded as certain that most of the aberrations discoverable in Codexes of the Sacred Text have arisen in the first instance from the merest inadvertency of the scribes.*"[25]

Then there is what the Dean refers to on page 24 as PURE ACCIDENT.[26] He writes:

> "*[It often happens that more causes than one are combined in the origin of the corruption in any one passage. In the following history of a blunder and of the fatal consequences that ensued upon it, only the first step was accidental. But much instruction may be derived from the initial blunder, and though the later stages in the history come under another head, they nevertheless illustrate the effects of early accident, besides throwing light upon parts of the discussion which are yet to come.]*"[27]

THE CAUSE WHICH HAS AFFECTED OUR TRANSLATIONS TODAY

---

[24] John William Burgon, The Causes of the Corruption of the Traditional Text of the Holy Gospels, Christian Classics Ethereal Library, pdf, http://www.ccel.org/ccel/burgon/corruption.toc.html

[25] http://www.ccel.org/ccel/burgon/corruption.toc.html pdf, p. 22.

[26] Ibid, p.24

[27] Ibid, p. 24

The Dean has much more to say on the subject of corruption, but we will hurry on to Chapter Thirteen of *THE CAUSES OF CORRUPTION CHIEFLY INTENTIONAL*. Here John Burgon writes:

> "*It has been shewn with sufficient clearness, I trust, in the course of the foregoing chapters, that the number of distinct causes to which various readings may reasonably be attributed is even extraordinary. But there remains after all an alarmingly large assortment of textual perturbations which absolutely refuse to fall under any of the heads of classification already enumerated. They are not to be accounted for on any ordinary principle. And this residuum of cases it is, which occasions our present embarrassment. They are in truth so exceedingly numerous; they are often so very considerable; they are, as a rule, so very licentious; they transgress to such an extent all regulations; they usurp so persistently the office of truth and faithfulness, that we really know not what to think about them. Sometimes we are presented with gross interpolations,—apocryphal stories: more often with systematic lacerations of the text, or transformations as from an angel of light. We are constrained to inquire, How all this can possibly have come about?*"[28]

On page 149 John Burgon continues by saying:

> "*It is found therefore that Satan could not even wait for the grave to close over St. John. 'Many' there were already who taught that CHRIST had not come in the flesh. Gnosticism was in the world already. St. Paul denounces it by name and significantly condemns the wild fancies of its professors, their dangerous speculations as well as their absurd figments. Thus he predicts and condemns their pestilential teaching in respect of meats and drinks and concerning matrimony.*
>
> "*In his Epistle to Timothy he relates that Hymeneus and Philetus taught that the resurrection was past already. What wonder if a flood of impious teaching broke loose*

---

[28] http://www.ccel.org/ccel/burgon/corruption.toc.html P. 148.

on the Church when the last of the Apostles had been gathered in, and another generation of men had arisen, and the age of Miracles was found to be departing if it had not already departed, and the loftiest boast which any could make was that they had known those who had [seen and heard the Apostles of the Lord].

"The 'grievous wolves' whose assaults St. Paul predicted as imminent, and against which he warned the heads of the Ephesian Church, did not long 'spare the flock.' Already, while St. John was yet alive, had the Nicolaitans developed their teaching at Ephesus and in the neighboring Church of Pergamos. Our risen LORD in glory announced to His servant John that in the latter city Satan had established his dwelling-place. Nay, while those awful words were being spoken to the Seer of Patmos, the men were already born who first dared to lay their impious hands on the Gospel of CHRIST."

"No sooner do we find ourselves out of Apostolic lines and among monuments of the primitive age than we are made aware that the sacred text must have been exposed at that very early period to disturbing influences which, on no ordinary principles, can be explained. Justin Martyr, Irenaeus, Origen, Clement of Alexandria, among the Fathers: some Old Latin MSS. 450, the Bohairic and Sahidic, and coming later on, the Curetonian and Lewis,—among the Versions: of the copies Codd.

"B and Aleph, and above all, coming later down still, Cod. D:—these venerable monuments of a primitive age occasionally present us with deformities which it is worse than useless to extenuate,—quite impossible to overlook. Unauthorized appendixes,—tasteless and stupid amplifications,—plain perversions of the meaning of the Evangelists,—wholly gratuitous assimilations of one Gospel to another,—the unprovoked omission of passages of profound interest and not unfrequently of high doctrinal import:—How are such phenomena as these to be accounted for? Again, in one quarter, we light upon a systematic mutilation of the text so extraordinary that it is as if some one had amused himself by running his pen through every clause which was not absolutely

necessary to the intelligibleness of what remained. In another quarter we encounter the thrusting in of fabulous stories and apocryphal sayings which disfigure as well as encumber the text.—How will any one explain all this?"[29]

But wait one minute, Mr. Burgon, you mentioned B and Aleph. Are not these manuscripts two of the oldest manuscripts in existence and are they not the primary Texts relied upon by Westcott and Hort and even by some of today's scholars?

MANUSCRIPTS B and ℵ ARE THE RESULT OF INTENTIONAL CORRUPTION

Not wanting to weary the reader, please allow John Burgon to elucidate more on the subject of manuscript age and corruption. Underlining and emphasis has been added to stress what Brother Burgon writes concerning manuscripts B and Aleph:

"Let me however at the risk of repeating what has been already said dispose at once of an uneasy suspicion which is pretty sure to suggest itself to a person of intelligence after reading what goes before. If the most primitive witnesses to our hand are indeed discovered to bear false witness to the text of Scripture,—whither are we to betake ourselves for the Truth? And what security can we hope ever to enjoy that any given exhibition of the text of Scripture is the true one? Are we then to be told that in this subject-matter the maxim 'id verius quod prius' does not hold? that the stream instead of getting purer as we approach the fountain head, on the contrary grows more and more corrupt?

"Nothing of the sort, I answer. The direct reverse is the case. ***Our appeal is always made to antiquity; and it is nothing else but a truism to assert that the oldest reading is also the best.*** *A very few words will make this matter clear; because a very few words will suffice to explain a circumstance already adverted to which it is necessary to keep always before the eyes of the reader.*

---

[29] http://www.ccel.org/ccel/burgon/corruption.toc.html P. 150.

*"The characteristic note, the one distinguishing feature, of all the monstrous and palpable perversions of the text of Scripture just now under consideration is this:—that they are never vouched for by the oldest documents generally, but only by a few of them,—two, three, or more of the oldest documents being observed as a rule to yield conflicting testimony (which in this subject-matter is **in fact contradictory**). In this way **the oldest witnesses nearly always refute one another, and indeed dispose of one another's evidence almost as often as that evidence is untrustworthy**. And now I may resume and proceed."*

"I say then that it is an adequate, as well as a singularly satisfactory explanation of the greater part of those gross deprivations of Scripture which admit of no legitimate excuse, to attribute them, however remotely, to those licentious free-handlers of the text who are declared by their contemporaries to have falsified, mutilated, interpolated, and in whatever other way to have corrupted the Gospel; whose blasphemous productions of necessity must once have obtained a very wide circulation: and indeed will never want some to recommend and uphold them. What with those who like Basilides and his followers invented a Gospel of their own:—what with those who with the Ebionites and the Valentinians interpolated and otherwise perverted one of the four Gospels until it suited their own purposes:—what with those who like Marcion shamefully maimed and mutilated the inspired text:—__there must have been a large mass of corruption festering in the Church throughout the immediate post-Apostolic age.__ But even this is not all. There were those who like Tatian constructed Diatessarons, or attempts to weave the fourfold narrative into one,—'Lives of CHRIST,' so to speak;—and productions of this class were multiplied to an extraordinary extent, and as we certainly know, not only found their way into the remotest corners of the Church, but established themselves there. And will any one affect surprise if occasionally a curious scholar of those days was imposed upon by the confident assurance that by no means were those many sources of light to be indiscriminately rejected, but that there must be some

truth in what they advanced?

"In a singularly uncritical age, the seductive simplicity of one reading,—the interesting fullness of another,—the plausibility of a third,—was quite sure to recommend its acceptance amongst those many eclectic recensions which were constructed by long since forgotten Critics, from which the most depraved and worthless of our existing texts and versions have been derived. Emphatically condemned by Ecclesiastical authority, and hopelessly outvoted by the universal voice of Christendom, buried under fifteen centuries, the corruptions I speak of survive at the present day chiefly in that little handful of copies which, calamitous to relate, the school of Lachmann and Tischendorf and Tregelles look upon as oracular: and in conformity with which many scholars are for refashioning the Evangelical text under the mistaken title of 'Old Readings.' And now to proceed with my argument."[30]

Burgon's argument is that as:

"Numerous as were the heresies of the first two or three centuries of the Christian era, they almost all agreed in this;—that they involved a denial of the eternal Godhead of the SON of Man: denied that He is essentially very and eternal GOD. This fundamental heresy found itself hopelessly confuted by the whole tenor of the Gospel, which nevertheless it assailed with restless ingenuity: and many are the traces alike of its impotence and of its malice which have survived to our own times. It is a memorable circumstance that it is precisely those very texts which relate either to the eternal generation of the SON,—to His Incarnation,—or to the circumstances of His Nativity, —which have suffered most severely, and retain to this hour traces of having been in various ways

---

[30] http://www.ccel.org/ccel/burgon/corruption.toc.html , pdf, PP 150, 151.

tampered with."[31]

This is a very important point and that is that in the days immediately after the Gospels were written and in the early days of the churches, there were those who denied the eternal Sonship and deity of the Lord Jesus Christ!

There is so much to mull over in what has just been quoted from John Burgon on the corruption of Scripture, but only two things will be noted here and they are; Origen and Codex B. Burgon says: *"Lachmann, Tischendorf, Tregelles, Alford, Westcott and Hort, have all in turn bowed to the authority of Cod. B and Origen."*[32] This is very important to know in the Text issue and its corruption.

ORIGEN AND CORRUPTION
OF THE TEXT

As to Origen, Burgon writes:

> *"Above all, it is to be inferred that **licentious and rash Editors of Scripture,—among whom Origen may be regarded as a prime offender**,—must have deliberately introduced into their recensions many an unauthorized gloss, and so given it an extended circulation. (Emphasis added)"*[33]

Edward Miller writes that:

> *"Though Origen was no Arian, yet a later offshoot of the same great stock was found in Arianism. And no one can wonder if a line of inferior texts can be traced—with a class of readings which were afterwards thrown aside in the Church—from Origen onwards till the time of the close of the Arian heresy. Debased doctrine, and readings of Holy Scripture afterwards to be rejected,*

[31] Jhttp://www.ccel.org/ccel/burgon/corruption.toc.html, pdf, PP 151, 152.

[32] Ibid, Page 84.

[33] http://www.ccel.org/ccel/burgon/corruption.toc.html , Page 76.

would naturally go hand in hand."[34]

In fact:

> *"The employment of corrupt manuscripts has been detected in the writings of Clement of Alexandria, the immediate predecessor of Origen in the Catechetical School, by Dean Burgon* (Emphasis added)."[35]

It is often true that as goes teacher so goes student!

As for Codex B, Burgon writes:

> *"The prejudice which would erect Codices B and Aleph into an authority for the text of the New Testament from which there shall be no appeal:—the superstitious reverence which has grown up for one little cluster of authorities, to the disparagement of all other evidence wheresoever found; this, which is for ever landing critics in results which are simply irrational and untenable, must be unconditionally abandoned, if any real progress is to be made in this department of inquiry."*[36]

Burgon goes on to say:

> *"What are we to think of guides like אBCD, which are proved to be utterly untrustworthy?"*[37]

The answer to this of course would be *"not much"* after reading more of what John Burgon has to say about them. So let's see what Brother Burgon has further to say about these two corrupters.

Of Matthew 5:44 Burgon says:

> *"One more indication has been obtained of the corruptness of the text which Origen employed,*

---

[34] Edward Miller, A GUIDE TO THE TEXTUAL CRITICISM OF THE NEW TESTAMENT, pdf. p.78.

[35] Ibid.

[36] http://www.ccel.org/ccel/burgon/corruption.toc.html, pdf, PP 76, 77.

[37] http://www.ccel.org/ccel/burgon/corruption.toc.html, pdf, p.86.

concerning which he is so strangely communicative, and of which B are the chief surviving examples; and the probability has been strengthened that when these are the sole, or even the principal witnesses, for any particular reading, that reading will prove to be corrupt."[38]

Burgon again writes that ". . . *Origen, who was but too well acquainted with Codexes of the same depraved character as the archetype of B and* א. . ."[39] CORRUPT AND **DEPRAVED** is what Burgon thought of Westcott and Hort's favorite manuscript!

On page 150 Burgon says:

"No sooner do we find ourselves out of Apostolic lines and among monuments of the primitive age than we are made aware that the sacred text must have been exposed at that very early period to disturbing influences which, on no ordinary principles, can be explained. Justin Martyr, Irenaeus, Origen . . . among the Fathers: some Old Latin MSS.450, the Bohairic and Sahidic, and coming later on, the Curetonian and Lewis,—among the Versions: of the copies Codd. B and א: *and above all, coming later down still, Cod. D:—these venerable monuments of a primitive age occasionally present us with deformities which it is worse than useless to extenuate,—quite impossible to overlook." Note he says the favorite manuscripts of Westcott, Hort and many others; have "DEFORMITIES"! This is not a good recommendation!!*

However, these deformities did not keep Westcott, Hort, and others from following B and א when the majority of other manuscripts disagreed. In a footnote on page 76, Burgon says:

"What enabled the Revisers, with Lachmann, Tischendorf, Tregelles, Westcott and Hort, to recognize in a reading, which is the peculiar property of B, the genuine language of the HOLY GHOST? Is not a superstitious reverence for B and א *betraying for ever*

---

[38] Ibid, Page 114.

[39] Ibid, Page 116.

people into error?" There it is, a "superstitious reverence" which has led others since into translation error! If the base of the translation is corrupt the translation itself will be corrupt!!!

Then we read that because Codex אBCDL all omit καὶ η᾽ λαλιά σου oʼμοιάζει from Mark 14:70 "... *Lachmann, Tischendorf, Tregelles, Alford, Westcott and Hort entirely eject these five precious words from St. Mark's Gospel...*"[40] John Burgon then defends why these words were in the Original Words that God breathed.

There is much more that could be written and quoted supporting the fact that very soon after the New Testament was finished, there were those who began an INTENTIONAL CORRUPTION of the Words of God. Edward Miller gives seven passages affected by the INTENTIONAL CORRUPTERS. Those passages are[41]:

I.   The Last Twelve Verses of St. Mark's Gospel.

II.   The First Word from the Cross. St. Luke 23: 34

III.   The Record of the Strengthening Angel, the Agony, and the Bloody Sweat. Luke 22: 43, 44

IV.   The Angelic Hymn. Luke 2: 14

V.   The Doxology in the Lord's Prayer. Matthew 6: 13

VI.   The Son of God's Eternal Existence in Heaven. John 3: 13

VII.   God Manifested in the Flesh. 1 Timothy 3:16

So in conclusion, it was very soon after the writing of the Gospels, the corrupters were busy about their work! Their work was adding to and subtracting from the Words of God which God Himself had warned men not to do. *"For I testify unto every man that heareth the words of the prophecy of this book: If any man shall add unto these things, God shall add unto him the plagues that are written in this book"* Revelation 22:18.

The result of these corrupters was manuscripts B, Aleph and a few others. It was mainly B and Aleph that Westcott and Hort used to establish their Greek

---

[40] http://www.ccel.org/ccel/burgon/corruption.toc.html, pdf, Page 91.

[41] Edward Miller, A GUIDE TO THE TEXTUAL CRITICISM OF THE NEW TESTAMENT, pdf. PP. 125 – 137.

Text, and, unfortunately, it is basically this text used for all modern English and foreign translations of the Scriptures.

However in spite of the corrupters and their corrupted manuscripts,

> *"The position of the Holy Scriptures as inspired by God the Holy Ghost must never be allowed to pass out of recollection. The great Inspirer of the Writings is also Himself the great Guide of the Church. Accordingly,* **the overruling care exercised by Him** *according to promise is a factor all through the history which must ever be borne in mind. Not of course that evil has been excluded from coexisting along with the good—such is the universal experience: but nevertheless the Church, as the 'Witness and Keeper of Holy Writ,' has, under His direction, cast out the evil from time to time, and has kept to a generally defined course. Serious errors might have been committed in the transmission of the works of Homer, or of Thucydides, or of Aristotle: and indeed many of the books of the last of these are supposed to have perished. But it can hardly be conceived that the Holy Ghost, after communicating His Inspiration in the composition of books, would in the midst of* **His overruling care** *have allowed those books to be varied according to changing winds of human opinion and human action, without* **the maintenance throughout of a form mainly at least free from error. It can scarcely be but that a succession of copies pure from any great corruption must have existed, and existed too in predominance, all down the Church's history** *(Emphasis added)."*[42]

In spite of the corruption performed on God's Words, God PRESERVED HIS WORDS. That is the subject of the next Chapter and because of that Divine superintending over the **PRESERVATION** of God's inspired Words, we today may hold ". . . *forth the word of life* . . ." Philippians 2:16.

---

[42] Edward Miller, A GUIDE TO THE TEXTUAL CRITICISM OF THE NEW TESTAMENT, pdf. p. 66.

CHAPTER THREE

BIBLE PRESERVATION

"While the Bible clearly teaches the ultimate indestructibility of the verbal revelation of God (Matthew 24:35; 1 Peter 1:25), it does not tell how and where the written manuscript lineage of that Word is preserved. We believe that God has providentially preserved His word in the many manuscripts, fragments, versions, translations, and copies of the Scriptures that are available, and ***that by diligent study, comparison, and correlation, the original text (words) can be ascertained*** *(Emphasis added)."*[43]

One wonders what manipulation those who make statements like that above do with these verses.

- Psalm 12:6-7 *"The words of the LORD* are pure words: as silver tried in a furnace of earth, purified seven times. 7 *Thou shalt keep them*, O LORD, thou shalt *preserve them* from this generation *for ever."*

- Psalm 119:89 *"forever ... thy word* is settled in heaven"

- Psalm 119:160 "every one of thy righteous judgments endureth *for ever"*

- Psalm 119:152 "thy testimonies ... thou hast founded them *forever"*

- Isaiah 40:8 *The grass withereth, the flower fadeth: but the word of our God shall stand for ever.*

- Matthew 5:18 "one jot or one tittle *shall in no wise pass"*

- Matthew 24:35 *"Heaven and earth shall pass away, but my words shall not pass away."*

---

[43] William W. Combs, THE PRESERVATION OF SCRIPTURE, *DBSJ* 5 (Fall 2000): 3–44, p. 11, pdf.

- Mark 13:31 "Heaven and earth shall pass away: but *my words shall not pass away.*"

- John 10: 35 *"The scripture cannot be broken."*

- 1 Peter 1:23 *"Being born again, not of corruptible seed, but of incorruptible, by the word of God which liveth and abideth for ever."*

- 1 Peter 1:25 *"But the word of the Lord endureth for ever."*

- Revelation 1:3 *"Blessed is he that readeth, and they that hear the words of this prophecy, and keep those things which are written therein. . ."*

Were the Words of God ever lost, and if so, can they ever be recovered? Has the Lord provided the present-day believer a copy of His original Words and have those Words been brought across accurately into an English Bible? Thus far, this paper has dealt with the INSPIRATION and the CORRUPTION that occurred soon after the Scriptures were completed. However, in spite of some men's intentional corrupting of God's Words, God was still in control. On the following page, is an illustration of God's PRESERVATION of His INSPIRED Words.

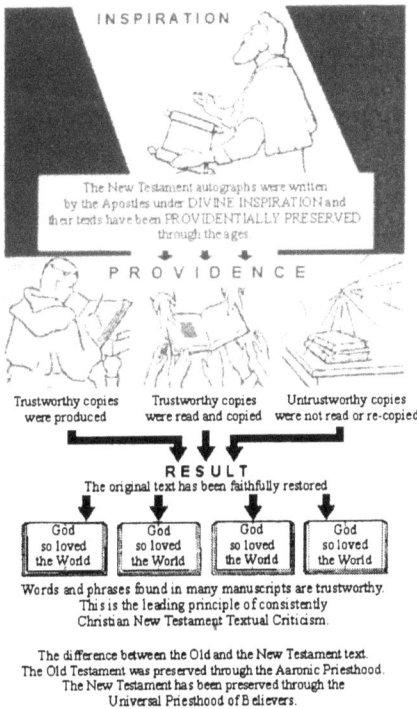

INSPIRATION

The New Testament autographs were written
by the Apostles under DIVINE INSPIRATION and
their texts have been PROVIDENTIALLY PRESERVED
through the ages.

PROVIDENCE

| Trustworthy copies were produced | Trustworthy copies were read and copied | Untrustworthy copies were not read or re-copied |

RESULT
The original text has been faithfully restored

| God so loved the World | God so loved the World | God so loved the World | God so loved the World |

Words and phrases found in many manuscripts are trustworthy.
This is the leading principle of consistently
Christian New Testament Textual Criticism.

The difference between the Old and the New Testament text.
The Old Testament was preserved through the Aaronic Priesthood.
The New Testament has been preserved through the
Universal Priesthood of Believers.

(E F Hills, Believing Bible Study, 11.
Used by permission of The Christian Research Press, Des Moines, Iowa, USA.)

The original manuscripts were never lost, but they were worn out through numerous copying so they could be shared among His churches. These copies were copied and those copies were copied. So the question is, did God by His providence preserve His Words via those copies produced from those original God breathed-out Words? My answer is, yes, He did. But some will ask the question, where are those Words today? The *Baptist Bulletin* of June 2011, says:

> "*None of these manuscripts exists today. The Greek and Hebrew manuscripts that we have are various copies produced by scribes through the ages.*"[44]

Yes, that is true and with the true copies there were also corrupt copies. Dr. Floyd Jones wrote in *WHICH VERSION IS THE BIBLE* that:

---

[44] http://baptistbulletin.org/?p=16799

"Corruption of the New Testament text had begun by the time of Paul. The following was preserved for us by the Holy Spirit through Paul in 2 Corinthians 2:17: "For we are not as many, which corrupt the word of God. . ."

"It is so very true that Bible corruption, beginning in the Garden of Eden, was out of control as early as the time of Paul. In other words, when the original apostles were here, there were already problems over the purity of the Bible text. This is confirmed and enlarged upon in 2 Corinthians 4:2: "But we (implied, vs 1) have renounced the hidden things of dishonesty, not walking in craftiness, nor handling the word of God deceitfully; . . ."[45]

So, from the first century on, there has been the pure original Words of God handed down in copy after copy and then there were also the corrupt words. The churches knew which were the pure Words of God and consistently used them. Howbeit, the corrupters were not satisfied, so in the 1800's two men (Westcott and Hort) devised a system by which they categorized these copies into families or Text-Types. Westcott and Hort also collaborated with others and finally published what is known as the Critical Greek Text.

This labeling of the Text–Types by Westcott and Hort puts it thusly as:
*"The **Majority Text** is a group of Greek New Testament manuscripts also described as **Byzantine Text-type**. These manuscripts form the basis for the **Textus Receptus**, a group of printed editions of the Greek New Testament text used by translators of the KJV and NKJV. Many KJV advocates believe the Textus Receptus is the best available Greek text. The **Alexandrian Text-type** is a group of Greek New Testament manuscripts that are older than the Majority Text, dating as early as the second or third century after Christ. Other groups of manuscripts are known as **Caesarean Text-type** and **Western Text-type**."*[46]

---

[45] FLOYD NOLAN JONES, WHICH VERSION IS THE BIBLE, pdf., pp. 13, 14.

[46] http://baptistbulletin.org/?p=16799

Are all of these text-types the Words of God? Some say:

> *"While scholars continue to discuss the merits of various Greek manuscripts, believers can be assured that their English Bible is an accurate translation. We believe our English translations are the Word of God."*[47]

One might ask, then, that if there are different families or text–types, there must be differences in the translations produced from them.

WE MUST REMEMBER THAT IF THEY ARE DIFFERENT THEY ARE NOT THE SAME!

Well, these differences are not a worry to some. They say:

> *"... God verbally inspired the original manuscripts of Scripture without error and without omission, but... He has preserved His Word through manuscripts that have some differences. I do not always know which reading reflects the original wording of a passage, but I do know that all of these readings reflect doctrine taught* <u>*somewhere*</u> *in the Bible and that none of these differences change what God's Word teaches. I can trust the Bible in my hands to be the Word of God."*[48]

Note the word **SOMEWHERE**! This is what I call the middle of the road view of preservation. Another, who takes this middle of the road outlook, states it this way saying:

> *"... the Scriptures have been preserved in the totality of the biblical manuscripts (Hebrew, Aramaic, and Greek)."*[49]

As Daniel Wallace says:

---

[47] http://baptistbulletin.org/?p=16799

[48] http://www.faith.edu/component/preachit/message/the-preservation-of-scripture/read?Itemid=0

[49] William W. Combs, THE PRESERVATION OF SCRIPTURE, *DBSJ* 5 (Fall 2000): 3–44, pdf, page 6.

> *"Thus the differences between the New Testament of the King James Version, for example, and that of the New American Standard Version are not just differences in the English; there are also differences in the Greek text behind the English—in fact, __over 5,000 differences!__"*[50]

Now that is a lot of differences and the text underlying the ASV is in constant flux! For instance the Greek text my Greek professor used was the UBS Greek New Testament 2nd Edition. The UBS is now on its 4th revised edition. According to the UBS website, this 4th edition is:

> *"is identical with that of the 26th and 27th editions of Novum Testamentum Graece by Nestle-Aland except for some minor punctuation differences."*[51]

This Critical Text is very fluid to say the least or it would not be forever changing. So will these people who have swallowed and followed the thinking of Westcott and Hort ever find the Words of God? Probably not!

However, the Dean Burgon Society (DBS), of which I am a member, gives one confidence in stating that:

> *"We believe that the Texts which are the closest to the original autographs of the Bible are the Traditional Masoretic Hebrew Text for the Old Testament, and the traditional Greek Text for the New Testament underlying the King James Version (as found in 'The Greek Text Underlying The English Authorized Version of 1611')."*[52]

Therefore there is only one Greek Text that can be said to be the Words of God and that is the Text underlying the King James Bible!

Furthermore, the Dean Burgon Society states that as a society it believes:

> *". . . that the King James Version (or Authorized Version) of the English Bible is a true, faithful, and accurate*

---

[50] Daniel B. Wallace, INSPIRATION, PRESERVATION, AND NEW TESTAMENT TEXTUAL CRITICISM, p. 1, pdf.

[51] http://www.ubs-translations.org/cat/biblical_texts/greek_scriptures_and_reference/new_testament/

[52] http://www.deanburgonsociety.org/DBS_Society/articles.htm

translation of these two providentially preserved Texts, which in our time has no equal among all of the other English Translations. The translators did such a fine job in their translation task that we can without apology hold up the Authorized Version of 1611 and say 'This is the WORD OF GOD!' while at the same time realizing that, in some verses, we must go back to the underlying original language Texts for complete clarity, and also compare Scripture with Scripture."[53]

On the Internet, there is http://kingjamesbiblesummit.org. Here one will find the following questions: [I want to make clear that I do not agree with some of the words used in this article. I make this clear on the next page.]

"Why do you use the King James Bible?

Please indicate below which statement most accurately describes your position on the King James.

Top of Form

Textus Receptus – *"I use it because it's the best translation available from the Textus Receptus, and the Textus Receptus is the best Greek manuscript family available."*

Preserved Word -- *"I use it because it is the preserved Word of God for the English-speaking world. The translators did a true and accurate translation which preserved the original Words in English. The printing errors and spelling standardization that have been fixed since 1611."*

Other:

Bottom of Form

The poll results are found at:
http://kingjamesbiblesummit.org/PollResults.php and they were:

> *"3% (19 votes) It's Comfortable -- I use it because that's what I am comfortable with (eg., mom and dad used it; the person who led me to the Lord used it; my pastor uses it; it's easier to memorize, etc.)*

> *"5 % (28 votes) Textus Receptus -- I use it because*

---

[53]

http://www.deanburgonsociety.org/DBS_Society/articles.htm

it's the best translation available from the Textus Receptus, and the Textus Receptus is the best Greek manuscript family available.

"10 % (58 votes) Preserved Word -- I use it because it is the accurate, preserved Word of God for the English-speaking world. Its words are not inspired, or God-breathed, but it is an accurate translation and most or all errors have been worked out of it over the years since 1611.

"56 % (311 votes) Preserved & Inspired Word -- I use it because it is the preserved, inspired Word of God for the English-speaking world. It is error-free and its words are of divine origin. God moved the minds and hands of the translators just as He did the authors of the original manuscripts, in order to ensure that His Word was accurately preserved. The printing errors and spelling standardization that have been fixed since 1611 do not negate its inspiration.

"5 % (27 votes) More accurate than the Greek--I use it because it is the Word of God. Its words are divinely inspired and supersede the Greek, so that we can find additional, new revelation in the English wording of the King James that does not exist in the Greek.

"20 % (112 votes) Other"

Now from this poll, it is seen the majority believed that the King James Bible is both the preserved AND inspired Word! It therefore should be noted that:

*"As the Bible uses it, the term 'inspiration' refers to the **writings**, not the **writers (2 Timothy 3:16-17)**; the **writers** are spoken of as being 'holy men of God' who were 'moved,' 'carried' or 'borne' along by the Holy Spirit (2 **Peter 1:21**) in such a definite way that their **writings** were supernaturally, plenarily, and verbally inspired, free from any error, infallible, and inerrant, as no other **writings** have ever been or ever will be inspired."*[54]

54

http://www.deanburgonsociety.org/DBS_Society/articles.htm

The King James Bible is a **TRANSLATION** of those <u>inspired preserved original Words of God</u>.

It is of utmost importance to understand that inspiration occurred but once! It is then the PRESERVATION of those inspired Words that we are concerned with. Those of the Dean Burgon Society believe that:

> ". . . *the Texts which are the closest to the original autographs of the Bible are the Traditional Masoretic Hebrew Text for the Old Testament, and the Traditional Greek Text for the New Testament underlying the King James Version (as found in 'The Greek Text Underlying The English Authorized Version of 1611').*"[55]

That Masoretic Hebrew text and the Greek Text underlying the King James Bible are the very preserved Hebrew, Aramaic, and Greek Words that God originally breathed out. Therefore:

> ". . . *the King James Version (or Authorized Version) of the English Bible is a true, faithful, and accurate translation of these two providentially preserved Texts, which in our time has no equal among all of the other English Translations. The translators did such a fine job in their translation task that we can without apology hold up the Authorized Version of 1611 and say 'This is the WORD OF GOD!' while at the same time realizing that, in some verses, we must go back to the underlying original language Texts for complete clarity, and also compare Scripture with Scripture.*"[56]

It may also be stated:

> ". . . *that all the verses in the King James Version belong in the Old and the New Testaments because they represent words . . . in the original texts, although there might be other renderings from the original languages which could also be acceptable to us today. For an exhaustive study of any of the words or verses in the Bible, we urge the student to return directly to the Traditional Masoretic*

---

[55] Ibid.

[56] http://www.deanburgonsociety.org/DBS_Society/articles.htm

> *Hebrew Text and the Traditional Received Greek Text*
> *rather than to any other translation for help."*[57]

So PRESERVATION has to do with the original inspired Words in Hebrew, Aramaic, and Greek. It does not apply to English or any other language into which the Words of God are translated. But it is often stated *"I do not know Hebrew or Greek. What do I do then?"* The answer: read and study your King James Bible for here you have an ACCURATE and FAITHFUL TRANSLATION of those inspired preserved Words!!! Of course, use lexicons, but never at the neglect of studying, meditating, and reading your King James Bible.

As Edward Hills wrote:

> *". . . God in His mercy did not leave His people to grope after the True New Testament Text. Through the leading of the Holy Spirit He guided them to preserve it during the manuscript period. God brought this to pass through the working of His preserving and governing providence. First, many trustworthy copies of the original New Testament manuscripts were produced by faithful scribes. Second, these trustworthy copies were read and recopied by true believers down through the centuries. Third, untrustworthy copies were not so generally read or so frequently recopied. Although they enjoyed some popularity for a time, yet in the long run they were laid aside and consigned to oblivion. Thus as a result of this special providential guidance the True Text won out in the end, and today we may be sure that the text found in the vast majority of the Greek New Testament manuscripts is a trustworthy reproduction of the divinely inspired Original Text. This is the text which was preserved by the God-guided usage of the Greek Church. Critics have called it the Byzantine text, thereby acknowledging that it was the text in use in the Greek Church during the greater part of the Byzantine period (452-1453). It is much better, however, to call this text the Traditional Text. When we call the text found in the majority of the Greek New Testament manuscripts the Traditional Text, we signify that this is the text which has been handed down by the*

---

[57] Ibid.

*God-guided tradition of the Church from the time of the
Apostles unto the present day."*[58]

Here I will quote Dr. Frederick Scrivener who said that our King James
Bible is: *". . . not a translation of any one Greek text then in existence. . . ."*[59]
In producing his Greek New Testament Dr. Scrivener:

> *". . . reasoned that 'between 1598 and 1611 no important
> edition appeared; so that Beza's fifth and last text of 1598
> was more likely than any other to be in the hands of the
> King James's revisers, and to be accepted by them as the
> best standard within their reach.' Where the English of
> the KJV differed from Beza's 1598 Greek edition, Dr.
> Scrivener (in about 162 places) used readings from
> previous Greek editions of the Received Text. He kept
> Beza's 1598 readings in about 59 places where the KJV
> had only Latin support."*[60]

One can believe by faith the critical Greek texts produced by the various
Bible societies represent the Words of God or one can by faith believe as the
Dean Burgon Society believes:

> *". . . that Scrivener's Greek Text which underlies our King
> James Bible is the closest to the original New
> Testament."*[61]

Even if one is not proficient in the Greek language of the Bible it is
wonderful to be able to hold in one's hands that volume containing the original,
inspired, preserved Words of God from which the King James Bible was
translated!!!

---

[58] Edward F. Hills, The King James Version Defended, p 6,
pdf.

[59] D. A. Waite, Jr., PREFACE to the "DOCTORED" NEW
TESTAMENT, The Bible For Today Press, 900 Park Avenue,
Collingswood, NJ 08108, 2003, p viii.

[60] Ibid.

[61] SCRIVENER'S ANNOTATED GREEK NEW
TESTAMENT, Dean Burgon Society Press, Box 354,
Collingswood, NJ 08108, 1999, Publisher's Foreword.

There is an old sales adage known as the KISS method; "Keep It Simple Stupid." So in this discussion on the Greek text; keep it simple. One believes the issue is either **SETTLED** on the fact that we have the Words of God preserved in the text underlying our King James Bible or one must continue to **SEARCH**, knowing their English Scriptures will continue to change just as their Critical Greek texts have.

Here is an example of how fluid the line of Critical-text-translated English Bibles are. It basically began in 1881 based on Westcott and Hort's Greek New Testament.

CRITICAL GREEK TEXT VERSIONS

1881 Revised Version.

1898 American Revised Version.

1901 American Standard Version

1952 Revised Standard Version.

1958 Berkeley Version (BV)

1970 New English Bible (NEB)

1971 New American Standard Bible (NAB)

1978 New International Version (NIV)

1996 NIV Inclusive Language (NIVI)

2001 English Standard Version (ESV)

These are just a sampling of those versions that have been spawned from the Critical Greek text. This stream flows from 1% of Greek manuscript evidence (fact). So with this 1% the **SEARCH** continues and the ESV is the latest result. The ESV is the flavor of the month for many fundamentalists and "conservative" new evangelicals. The ESV is based:

> ". . . on the Greek text in the 1993 editions of the Greek
> New Testament (4th corrected ed.), published by the
> United Bible Societies (UBS), and Novum Testamentum

Graece (27th ed.), edited by Nestle and Aland."[62]

As can be seen in the diagram below, it is in the stream of the Westcott and Hort tradition.

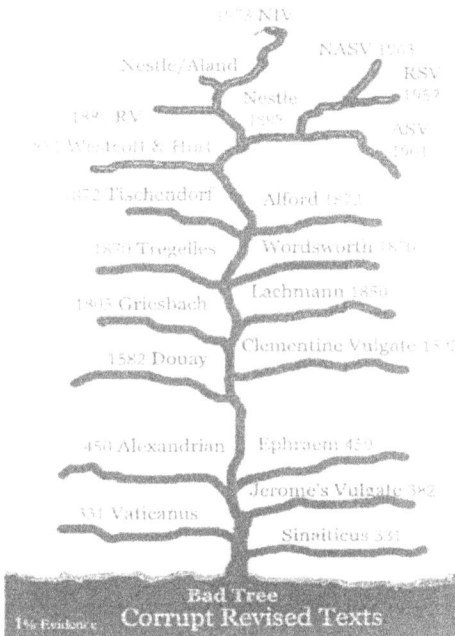

Chart above from D. A. Waite, Power Point Presentation to an annual Dean Burgon Society meeting.

---

[62] http://www.esv.org/esv/translation/about/

The King James Bible is in the stream flowing out of 99% of the manuscript evidence (fact) and both have a glorious heritage!

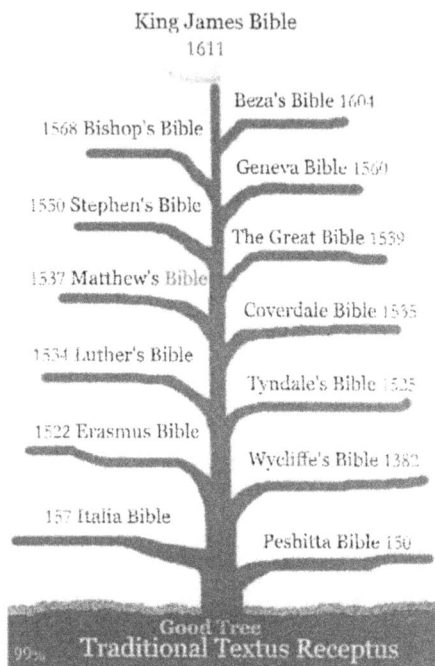

King James Bible
1611

Beza's Bible 1604

1568 Bishop's Bible

Geneva Bible 1560

1550 Stephen's Bible

The Great Bible 1539

1537 Matthew's Bible

Coverdale Bible 1535

1534 Luther's Bible

Tyndale's Bible 1525

1522 Erasmus Bible

Wycliffe's Bible 1382

157 Italia Bible

Peshitta Bible 150

Good Tree
99% Traditional Textus Receptus

[The above chart is from D. A. Waite, Power Point Presentation to an annual Dean Burgon Society annual meeting.]

In closing and in seeking to keep it simple, those who are saved by grace through **faith**, walk by **faith** and accept by **faith** and manuscript evidence (**fact**) that the Greek text underlying the King James Bible is the **PRESERVED** and **INSPIRED** Words of the **ORINGINAL INSPIRED** Words of God are **SETTLED** and rest in that assurance. On the other hand those who accept the minority Critical Greek Text will continue to **SEARCH** and **SEARCH** and hopefully someday through restoration they will have a settled Bible?

A school that fits into the still **SEARCHING** group and is **the leader** of the fundamentalist searching schools, is the one-time bastion of fundamentalism Bob Jones University (BJU). BJU states that they:

> "... *believe in the verbal, plenary inspiration of the Bible in the original manuscripts, and we believe that God has supernaturally preserved every one of His inspired words for us today. However, from the founder to the present administration, we have never taken the position that there can be only one good translation in the English language.*"[63]

Therefore pick and choose the version that fits!

BJU, Detroit Baptist Seminary, Faith Baptist Bible College and Theological Seminary and others take what may be described as the middle-of-the-road view, or the pick-and-choose position. To these people the Bible is preserved, but all the English translations, no matter how much they differ between themselves, are the Words of God. This position will **never** lead to a **SETTLED** position on an English translation, or for that matter, any language translation.

May the Lord help some **SEARCHING** reader to prayerfully come to that **SETTLED** position and **SIMPLY** rest in the knowledge that in our hands today we have a faithful and trustworthy translation in the King James Bible from the PRESERVED AND INSPIRED Words breathed out from God!

In the next chapter, the subject of translating will be considered. You can see at the bottom of this page an illustration of how the New Testament in the King James Bible was translated from Scrivener's Greek New Testament.

---

[63]http://www.bju.edu/communities/ministries-schools/position-statements/translation.php

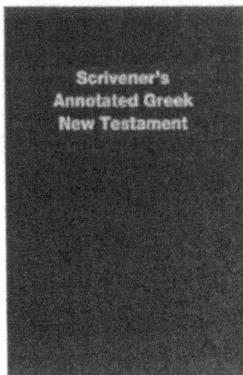
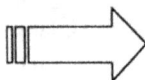
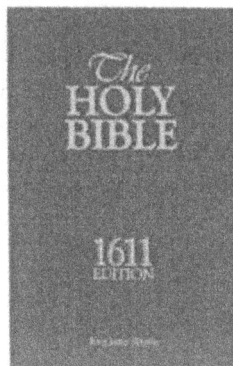

CHAPTER FOUR

BIBLE TRANSLATION

Psalm 11:3 *"If the foundations be destroyed, what can the righteous do?"* The Hebrew, Aramaic, and Greek Texts are the very foundation of the Words of God, the Bible. Thus far in this book, the main object has been to identify and defend the Greek Text that is an exact copy of those original Words of the New Testament. This is done so believers may have **confidence** in the Bible which they hold in their hands. Note that:

> *"During His earthly life, the Lord Jesus Christ appealed unreservedly to the very words of the Old Testament text (Matthew 22:42-45; John 10:34-36), thus indicating His* **confidence** *that this text had been accurately transmitted (Emphasis added)."*[64]

For our New Testament:

> *"One of the leading principles of the Protestant Reformation was the sole and absolute authority of the holy Scriptures. The New Testament text in which early Protestants placed such implicit* **confidence** *was the Textus Receptus (Received Text) which was first printed in 1516 under the editorship of Erasmus and only slightly modified in subsequent editions during the 16th and 17th centuries (Emphasis added)."*[65]

The resultant English translation will "**usually**" (why I use this word, note page 3, first paragraph of this chapter) bear the marks of the foundational Greek

---

[64] Jack Moorman, FOREVER SETTLED, pdf, Page 3.

[65] Ibid. page 148

Text and the translator's principles and techniques. This writer is not a Greek student nor is he a translator, so therefore I will seek to keep it simple. However, this keeping it simple is not necessarily for the reader but for the writer. A good book by a fundamentalist covering the principles and techniques of translating is Dr. H. D. Williams' book *WORD-FOR-WORD TRANSLATING of THE RECEIVED TEXTS* and is available through Amazon, the Bible For Today, and the Dean Burgon Society.

Webster's 1828 dictionary says the word *"translate"* comes from the Latin "L. *translatus*, from *transfero*; *trans*, over, and *fero*, to bear." Therefore to translate means to bear or carry over from one language to another. In the case of the English New Testament that is to bear or carry over from the Greek into the English. Dr. D. A. Waite has coined the term verbal plenary translating which:

> "... *taking all of the inspired, preserved Words of God*
> *(the canon of the Bible known as the Received Texts) into*
> *a receptor language using the principles of syntax.*"[66]

Hopefully, the prior three chapters have convinced the readers that they may **rest** in the knowledge that the Text underlying the New Testament of the King James Bible is that Text not just <u>containing</u> the Words of God but ARE those original Words of God! However, and sadly, many of the "fundamental" schools and church fellowships do not agree as do most Bible Societies. Dr. Phil Stringer states that:

> "*By the 1930's the Critical Text had complete dominance*
> *in all American Bible Societies.*"[67]

Some of our fundamental brethren seem to forget that there are over FIVE THOUSAND DIFFERENCES between the Text underlying our King James

---

[66] H. D. Williams, WORD-FOR-WORD-TRANSLATING of THE RECEIVED TEXTS, The Bible For Today Press, 900 Park Ave., Collingswood, NJ 08108, USA, Page xx.

[67] H. D. Williams, WORD-FOR-WORD-TRANSLATING of THE RECEIVED TEXTS, The Bible For Today Press, 900 Park Ave., Collingswood, NJ 08108, USA, Page 162.

Bible and the Critical Text.[68] These differences amount to 1 and 2 Peter missing from the new versions. That is pretty significant! Therefore it must be understood that if they are different they are not the same[69] and the reader of such a version has only a tentative Bible[70]!

Whether the translators say it or not, the basic foundation for all the new English versions, other than the New King James, is the Westcott and Hort Greek text. The popular Bible for many "fundamentalists" and "conservative" evangelicals today is the English Standard Version (ESV). According to the ESV website, the ESV is based:

"... on the Greek text in the 1993 editions of the Greek New Testament (4th corrected ed.), published by the United Bible Societies (UBS), and Novum Testamentum Graece (27th ed.), edited by Nestle and Aland."[71]

Now I have the 2nd Edition of the UBS Greek Text before me which is in the family of the one used by the ESV translators. The USB 2nd Edition says on page 5 that the committee that produced this edition:

"carried out its work in four stages" and the first stage was "on the basis of Westcott and Hort's edition of the Greek New Testament. ... "

The ESV website tells the reader that:

"The words and phrases themselves grow out of the Tyndale-King James legacy, and most recently out of the RSV, with the 1971 RSV text providing the starting point for our work." It is also said the ESV "was commissioned for the **purpose of modifying RSV passages that conservatives had long disputed**: e.g., the RSV's Isaiah

---

[68] Daniel B. Wallace, INSPIRATION, PRESERVATION, AND NEW TESTAMENT TEXTUAL CRITICISM, p. 1, pdf.

[69] Appendix A

[70] Appendix B

[71] http://www.esv.org/esv/translation/about/

7:14 usage of the phrase "young woman" was changed back to "virgin". Unlike its cousin, it used only a small amount of gender-neutral language. (Emphasis added)"[72]

The ESV's Greek foundation can be traced back to the great granddaddy Greek Text of Westcott and Hort (WH). W & H along with others in the Convocation were told:

"to make as few alterations as possible, and to make no changes in the Received Text unless the evidence for them was decidedly preponderating. Nevertheless, they went on changing until they had altered the reading of the Greek text in 5,337 places, within a few hundred of those made by Westcott and Hort. Philip Schaff counted 36,191 corrections in the Revised Version, or four and a half to each verse."[73]

It is interesting to read (at least to this writer and that is why I used the word "__usually__" in the second paragraph, first page of this chapter) of the ESV's including certain passages omitted in the Greek Text from which it was translated. We read that:

"In 1971, the RSV Bible was re-released with the Second Edition of the Translation of the New Testament. Whereas in 1962 the translation panel had merely authorized a handful of changes, in 1971 they gave the New Testament text a thorough editing. This Second Edition incorporated Greek manuscripts not previously available to the RSV translation panel, namely, the Bodmer Papyri, published in 1956-61."

72

http://en.wikipedia.org/wiki/Revised_Standard_Version#Engli
sh_Standard_Version

[73] WILLIAM WALLACE EVERTS, THE WESTCOTT AND HORT TEXT UNDER FIRE, Page 5, pdf., originally published in the Journal of Theological Studies, vol. U. p. 602.

"*The most obvious changes were the restoration of Mark 16:9-20 (the long ending) and John 7:53-8:11 (in which Jesus forgives an adulteress) to the text (in 1946, they were put in footnotes). Also restored was Luke 22:19b-20, containing the bulk of Jesus' institution of the Lord's Supper. In the 1946-52 text, this had been cut off at the phrase "This is my body," and the rest had only been footnoted, since this verse did not appear in the original Codex Bezae manuscript used by the translation committee. The description of Christ's ascension in Luke 24:51 had the footnote ". . . and was carried up into heaven" restored to the text. Luke 22:43-44, which had been part of the text in 1946-52, was relegated to the footnote section because of its questionable authenticity; in these verses, an angel appears to Jesus in Gethsemane to strengthen and encourage Him before His arrest and crucifixion. <u>Many other verses were rephrased or rewritten for greater clarity and accuracy. Moreover, the footnotes concerning monetary values were no longer expressed in terms of dollars and cents but in terms of how long it took to earn each coin (the denarius was no longer defined as twenty cents but as a day's wage). The book of Revelation,</u> called "The Revelation to John" in the previous editions, was retitled 'The Revelation to John (The Apocalypse)'. Some of these changes to the RSV New Testament had already been introduced in **<u>the 1965-66 Catholic Edition, and their introduction into the Protestant edition</u>** was done to pave the way for the publication of the RSV Common Bible in 1973. (Underlining added)*"[74]

The Bodmer Papyri play an important part in the foundation of the ESV. Of the Bodmer Papyri we read that:

"*The year 1952 brought forth from the sands of Egypt a remarkably-intact 144-page papyrus containing the oldest*

---

[74]

http://en.wikipedia.org/wiki/Revised_Standard_Version#Engli sh_Standard_Version *manuscripts ever found. . . ."*[75]

Also consider that:

> *"The term 'Bodmer papyri' is the conventional designation of an important group of manuscripts (75 percent on papyrus and 25 percent on parchment, at least 950 folios) held by the Martin Bodmer Foundation, at Cologny, near Geneva. There are good reasons for thinking that these manuscripts were found together as a complete collection (perhaps a private library) in Upper Egypt; the great majority of them (81 percent) was acquired by the learned Swiss collector Martin Bodmer, for his library."*[76]

The Bodmer Papyri was found of all places in the sands of Egypt and because of its antiquity, those passages such as the longer ending of Mark and the John 7: 53–8: 11 are inserted back in the ESV. Here is a text out of the sands of Egypt that follows the Received Text! However, as Dr. Floyd Nolan Jones points out, that:

> *"During the early Christian centuries, Egypt was a land in which heresies were rampant. Indeed, Hills reports that the texts of all the Bodmer Papyri are error-ridden and have been tampered with, in part by Gnostic heretics."*[77]

Nevertheless,

> *"The papyri (around 200 A.D.), which dates 150 years before Vaticanus and Sinaiticus, support the Textus Receptus readings. This may come as somewhat of a shock to those familiar with the problem of textual criticism, as most have been informed that the early papyri are listed as Alexandrian or Western. True,*

75

http://solidarityassociation.com/index.php?option=com_content&view=section&layout=blog&id=21&Itemid=151

[76] RODOLPHE KASSER, BODMER PAPYRI, pdf, page 1.

[77] FLOYD NOLAN JONES, WHICH VERSION IS THE BIBLE, 2010, pdf, Page 173

*nevertheless the Chester Beatty and **Bodmer Papyri**, even though placed in those families, have many renderings which are strictly Syrian–strictly Textus Receptus. After a thorough study of P46, Gunther Zuntz concluded: 'A number of Byzantine readings, most of them genuine, which previously were discarded as 'late', are anticipated by P46.' Having several years earlier already acknowledged that with regard to the Byzantine New Testament 'Most of its readings existed in the second century,' Colwell noted Zuntz's remark and concurred. Many of these had been considered 'late readings,' but the papyri testify that they date back at least to the second century! (Emphasis added)"*[78]

If one had placed their confidence in the Received Text in the first place, these passages in Mark and John would never have been deleted for:

"The true text continued to circulate among the more lowly and humble classes of Christian folk virtually undisturbed by the influence of other texts. Moreover, because it was difficult for these less prosperous Christians to obtain new manuscripts, they put the ones they had to maximum use. Thus all these early manuscripts of the true text were eventually worn out. The papyri which do survive seem for the most part to be prestige-texts which were preserved in the libraries of ancient schools. According to Aland (1963), both the Chester Beatty and the Bodmer Papyri may have been kept at such an institution. But the papyri with the true text were read to pieces by the believing Bible students of antiquity. In the providence of God they were used by the Church. They survived long enough, however, to preserve the true (Traditional) New Testament text during this early period of obscurity and to bring it out into the period of triumph which followed."[79]

---

[78]Ibid., Page 158.

[79] JACK MOORMAN, FOREVER SETTLED, pdf, Page 50.

It should also be noted that the inclusion of Mark 16:9–20; John 7:53 ff., and other once "disputed" passages into the ESV are a **departure** from other English versions such as the New International Version (NIV). The translators of the NIV said:

> "*Mark 16:9 – [The most reliable early manuscripts and other ancient witnesses do not have Mark 16: 9–20.] John 7:53–[The earliest and most reliable manuscripts do not have John 7:53–8:11.]*"[80]

So here, we have the ESV with passages that were omitted from the NIV. Now, think about this. When older manuscripts are found that may dispute the longer ending of Mark and the woman taken in adultery, will there be a New English Standard Version? CAN ONE HAVE **CONFIDENCE** IN THE ENGLISH STANDARD VERSION?

I do not think one can have confidence in the ESV or any of the other new English versions. They all have a faulty foundation. If the foundation is faulty, the finished structure will be faulty! I am not a builder, but I did learn some years ago, that when building, you must make sure the foundation is solid and secure. One can only have real confidence in the structure if you know the foundation is correct.

So which NEW VERSION does one use? Can one EVER REST knowing that they have the Words of God in the English language if they vacillate from one new version to another? Can one now go to the ESV with confidence after using the NIV? If they are different, they are not the same.

The foundation of the ESV is basically the same as the NIV with a few tweaks, for we read on page **68** of *THE MAKING OF A CONTEMPORARY TRANSLATION:*

> "*What Greek text was used by the translators of the NIV New Testament? It was basically that found in the **United Bible Societies'** and **Nestle's** printed Greek New Testaments, which contain the latest and best Greek text*

---

[80] KENNETH L. BARKER, THE MAKING OF A CONTEMPORARY TRANSLATION, Hodder & Stoughton, 1987, page 48.

available (Emphasis added)."

REMEMBER, the ESV website says the ESV is based:

*". . . on the Greek text in the 1993 editions of the Greek New Testament (4th corrected ed.), published by the **United Bible Societies** (UBS), and Novum Testamentum Graece (27th ed.), edited by **Nestle** and Aland. (Emphasis added)"*[81]

Yes, there are differences in the final structure between the ESV and the NIV (for if they were the same, one of them would not be necessary) but the foundation of both is basically the same and it has produced structures that will not stand the test of time and give **REST** and **CONFIDENCE** to the souls of their readers and hearers!

---

[81] http://www.esv.org/esv/translation/about/

CHAPTER FIVE

YOUR DECISION

Joshua 24:15 ". . . choose you this day. . . "

Today there are a multitude of English versions all claiming to be the Bible, the Words of God. But are they? As we have sought to show, not all the new versions are even the same because of different principles and techniques that have been used for the translating of the New Testament.

Most proponents of the new versions such as the NIV and ESV have good words to say for the King James Bible. For instance one says:

> "*I love the King James Version (KJV). I was converted under it. My first memory verses were taken from the KJV. I have been blessed by it. And God still uses the KJV. The way of salvation can still be found in the KJV. But the KJV is not the best translation to use today. It served its purpose for its day. It was translated by godly men who did an excellent job with the tools they had and with the language of four centuries ago. Countless millions have been converted, sanctified, and nurtured through it. Thank God for that marvellously-used translation. But today the KJV will not do. . . .*"[82]

---

[82] EDWIN H. PALMER, THE MAKING OF A CONTEMPORARY TRANSLATION, Hodder & Stoughton, 1987, Chapter 14, Page 196.

With friends like this who needs enemies?

The advocates of the ESV say:

> *"The King James Version (KJV) was the standard Bible used by the English-speaking world for almost four centuries. It was the one Bible that united the Church, strengthened believers, and brought untold millions of souls to Christ. Its literary beauty helped to shape the English language more than any other printed work before or since. Adults and children studied it and committed its verses to memory. It is still among the top-selling Bibles on current bestseller lists. The translators of the KJV understood the value of the English translation work that had been done before their time, and they wisely referred to the earliest English Bible translations, dating back to William Tyndale's 1526 New Testament, in addition to the manuscripts in their original languages."*[83]

Nevertheless the ESV people continue by saying:

> *"The English language has changed over the centuries, and modern readers find the KJV's archaic words and sentence structures difficult to understand. Throughout the course of the twentieth century, it became clear that Bible readers needed a translation they could easily understand. . ."*[84]

Those at the ESV website also share the words of Alister McGrath:

> *"The true heirs of the King James translators are those who continue their task today, not those who declare it to have been definitively concluded in 1611."*[85]

Changing the Words of God is not concluded and should continue according to this statement which will never bring REST and CONFIDENCE in the Words of God. There will always be a need for another version!

---

[83] http://www.esv.org/esv/history/kjv/

[84] Ibid.

[85] http://www.esv.org/esv/history/kjv/

So the King James Bible was good enough for several hundred years, but not so much today! Times have changed, the English language has changed, plus older manuscripts have been discovered. Consequently, with all of this, there must be a new version. As a result, what Bible will you read, study, and have CONFIDENCE in? Is it the NIV that uses the Greek text that omits certain passages that are in the King James Bible because those passages are not in the "oldest and best manuscripts"? Or is it the ESV that is based basically on the same Greek text as the NIV but tweaks it with the Bodmer Papyri and therefore inserts many of those passages the NIV has omitted. Or is it the King James Bible which is based on the Received Greek text used by the churches long before the "oldest and best manuscripts" were brought into the light of day, and has not changed since 1611 other than eliminating the Apocrypha and old English spelling?

In which Bible will you **REST** your **CONFIDENCE**? The decision is yours, but REMEMBER, it does make a difference what Bible you read and study. Only one English Bible can be right; for **IF THEY ARE DIFFERENT THEY ARE NOT THE SAME**[86]!

---

[86] Appendix A

APPENDIX A

IF THEY ARE DIFFERENT THEY ARE NOT THE SAME

Psalm 12:6-7 *"The words of the LORD are pure words: as silver tried in a furnace of earth, purified seven times. Thou shalt keep them, O LORD, thou shalt preserve them from this generation for ever."*

Matthew 24:35 *"Heaven and earth shall pass away, but my words shall not pass away."*

The Bible-believing Christian believes the Bible is the very Word and Words of the Living God and it is THE foundation of the Christian faith. Yet, some Christians believe the English translation of the Bible a local church or individual uses is not a real issue. The article THE GARBC AND BIBLE TRANSLATIONS states that the General Association of Regular Baptist Churches (GARBC) believes:

"... *our English translations are the Word of God.*"[87]

Now exactly which English translation are they speaking of? Do they really BELIEVE **ALL** English translations are the Words of God!? We will find out a little later they do not believe all are.

For example, Amazon lists:

"... *the top ten in current sales in the USA (as of 8/17/2009) to be the NAB, NRSV, NIV, KJV, The Message, NASB, NLT, RSV, The Amplified Bible, and the*

---

[87] http://baptistbulletin.org/?p=16799

Orthodox Study Bible."[88]

However for the GARBC not all English translations are equal for we are informed from the THE GARBC AND BIBLE TRANSLATIONS article that:

*"In 2009 The GARBC **Council of Eighteen** added the ESV to the list of translations approved for authors to use in Regular Baptist Press publications. When the council began the policy in 1963, the list included the KJV, ASV, Berkeley Version, and Williams translation. This list was expanded through the years and now includes ASV, ESV, Holman Christian Standard Bible, NASB, NIV, New Scofield Bible, and Amplified Bible."*

Note from the paragraph just quoted, that this approval is for those who write for the GARBC's printing arm, Regular Baptist Press. Now for the *"Individual churches in fellowship with the GARBC adopt (or exclude) Bible translations without interference from any other ecclesiastical authority. The GARBC is not a denomination, so it does not formally approve or disapprove any action of its churches (including their translation choices)."*[89]

So at least for printing purposes, the GARBC Council of Eighteen does not really believe ALL *"English translations are the Word of God"* or surely they would simply approve ALL of the English translations for use in Regular Baptist Press publications.

It should also be noted that the GARBC's *"approval"* list is slightly different from Amazon's. Are those that appear on Amazon but not on the GARBC approval list not the Words of God? Hmmm.

Now, think about those English translations which the GARBC Council of Eighteen does approve. Do they ALL agree one with the other or are they DIFFERENT? For instance the New American Standard Version (NASV) has Mark 16:9–20 in brackets and a foot note telling the reader:

"Some of the oldest mss. do not contain vv. 9–20"

whereas the King James Bible has the verses without brackets and without a footnote.

Again in the NASV the verses 44 and 46 are bracketed in Mark Chapter 9 with a footnote telling the reader that these verses:

---

[88] http://en.wikipedia.org/wiki/English_translations_of_the_Bible

[89] http://baptistbulletin.org/?p=18067

"*. . . are identical with v. 48, are not found in the best ancient mss.*"

The King James Bible has the verses without brackets or footnote.

Then, in 1 Thessalonians 2:15, the NASV has "*the prophets*" rather than "*their own prophets*" as does the King James Bible. Lastly, consider Acts 8:37 which in the King James Bible says:

> "*And Philip said, If thou believest with all thine heart, thou mayest. And he answered and said, I believe that Jesus Christ is the Son of God.*"

However, in the NASV it has brackets around the verse and a note saying "Many mss. do not contain this verse." Which Bible is correct, the NASV or the King James Bible? Since they DIFFER are they the SAME?

So, from these examples, it is seen the NASV and the King James Bible differ. Therefore, it MUST be said that IF TWO THINGS ARE DIFFERENT THEY ARE NOT THE SAME! Hence, should an ISSUE be raised as to what English translation a church or person uses?

But, in raising this issue, must one be a Greek scholar? Some argue that:

> "***Few people in the KJV-only movement have the academic training to address issues of textual criticism.*** *While Edward Hills, Charles Surrett, and Thomas Strouse make an attempt to ground their arguments in real textual critical issues, most defenses of KJV-only ideas are confusing, poorly written, and weakly argued. These unsophisticated arguments seem to stir up the passions of uninformed Christians who fear that someone will take away their Bible.*"[90]

One can see which side the writer of this article, Jeff Straub, is on and it is definitely not as an advocate for the King James Bible. Straub says these proponents of the King James Bible, Hills, Surrett and Strouse only:

> "*make an attempt to ground their arguments in real textual critical issues.*"

How condescending. I do not know Brother Surrett, but Edward Hills was a true scholar as is Dr. Strouse!

---

[90] http://baptistbulletin.org/?p=16763

Then Straub tells the reader that other arguments by King James Bible advocates are:

> "*confusing, poorly written, and weakly argued*" and "*unsophisticated*" and only stirs "*up the passions of uninformed Christians who fear that someone will take away their Bible.*"

Is there something to be feared?   Where does a Christian go to be informed, if they do become aware that there just might be an issue?   Do they go only to people such as Straub and others that take his position?

This is a remarkable statement that Straub makes saying that these poor "*uninformed Christians who fear that someone will take away their Bible*" is not actually a real issue. Well, consider this. In Mark 16, in the *Revised Good News Edition*, (not approved by the GARBC Council of Eighteen) it follows the NASV and all the other English versions in telling the reader that:

> "*Some manuscripts and ancient translations do not have this ending to the Gospel (verses 9-20).*"

Is this taking "*away*" some words of the Bible from these "*uninformed Christians*" or not? ARE THESE VERSES TRUE OR NOT? IS THERE SOMETHING TO FEAR?

The Revised Good News Edition tells the reader that:

> "*Some manuscripts and ancient translations have this shorter ending to the Gospel in addition to the longer ending (verses 9-20).*"

Again, this is typical of all English translations that follow the Critical Greek text. Which is it, the longer or shorter ending? If one takes the shorter ending, are they losing part of their Bible? If the Christian accepts the longer reading, are they adding to the Words of God? What scholar may I go to for a definitive answer?

The scholars behind the RSV continue to change the RSV. In the 1971 Second Edition:

> "*The longer ending of Mark (16:9-20) and the account of the woman caught in adultery (Jn 7:53-8:11), are restored to the text, separated from it by a blank space and accompanied by informative notes describing the various arrangements of the text in the ancient*

authorities."[91]

Restoration of Scripture, blank spaces, and notes, certainly will give the reader confidence in their Bible! Or will it?

Is there a scholar living that advocates the use of only the King James Bible for the English-speaking world? Yes, there are many living today who support the superiority of the King James Bible. The one scholar Mr. Straub mentions a couple of times in his article, is Dr. D. A. Waite. Now, this is probably due to the fact that

> *"Waite is among the more educated men in fundamentalism with two earned doctorates, one, a Th.D. in Bible Exposition from Dallas Theological Seminary in 1955 and the other, in speech from Purdue in 1961."*[92]

However, this does not mean Straub and the GARBC Council of Eighteen believe Dr. Waite is correct on this issue. In the *"July/August 1974 issue"*[93] of the *Baptist Bulletin,* there appeared two opposing articles on English Bible translations:

> *"The KJV view was advocated by D. A. Waite, director of The Bible for Today ministry and member of a GARBC church. His article, 'In Defense of the New Testament Majority Text,' advocated a position that was falling out of favor among GARBC pastors, but his tone was respectful and scholarly. The article ran right next to L. Duane Brown's 'Evaluating and Appreciating the King James Bible,' an article that showed appreciation for the KJV but did not advocate an exclusive use of the Majority Text. Brown suggested that several modern translations were helpful to pastors and church members, while other modern translations were dangerous. By this point, the GARBC Council of Eighteen had already approved a list of modern translations to be used in materials published*

---

[91] http://www.ncccusa.org/newbtu/aboutrsv.html

[92] http://baptistbulletin.org/?p=16763

[93] Ibid.

by Regular Baptist Press."[94]

It is hence interesting to note that, in spite of the degrees and credentials Dr. Waite has, the GARBC Council of Eighteen **HAD ALREADY APPROVED** numerous English versions to use alongside the King James Bible. Consequently, scholarship and degrees is not the answer in persuading a man or a group of men that the King James Bible is the superior English translation for the English speaking world.

It has been said by some people that Dr. Waite's position:

"was falling out of favor among GARBC pastors."

Why is this? Is this because the schools these men attended used the Critical Greek Text? It is also most likely it was never mentioned that there was another Greek text. And other Greek text had been used by the churches long before the one they were using in Greek class was ever conceived of in the nineteenth century.

Today, many within the "conservative" Baptist churches are using the English Standard Version (ESV). Rodney J. Decker, professor of New Testament and Greek at Baptist Bible Seminary, Clarks Summit, Pa., says:

> *"The ESV is not a new, 'made from scratch' translation, but is the newest revision of a line of translations that goes back to Tyndale and the KJV. The KJV of 1611 was a revision of the 1568 Bishop's Bible, which was a revision of Matthew's Bible of 1537—which was essentially the completion and revision of Tyndale's work (1534). In subsequent years the KJV was revised and updated at least a half dozen times, though retaining the same name. Most KJV Bibles in print today are of the last revision of 1769. The next revision with a new name is the Revised Version of 1881, better known in America as the American Standard Version of 1901. This was followed by the Revised Standard Version of 1952. Some theological issues with the RSV made it unsatisfactory, but these have been corrected in the ESV, which is a revision of the RSV. 'Archaic language has been brought to current usage and significant corrections have been made in the translation*

of key texts' (ESV Preface)."[95]

No wonder the preachers coming out of the "conservative" schools do not know there is truly an issue, when professors say things like what Decker just wrote. The ESV is not a revision of anything that goes back to Tyndale but:

> *"is an evangelical revision of the Revised Standard Version that corrects the non-Christian interpretations of the RSV in the Old Testament and improves the accuracy throughout with more literal renderings. It also updates the language somewhat."*[96]

The ESV also *"follows the Greek text of the UBS 4th ed."*[97] THE ESV IS NO RELATIVE OF THE KING JAMES BIBLE!

As for the Revised Standard Version,

> *"The translation panel used the 17th edition of the Nestle-Aland Greek text for the New Testament. . . ."*[98]

Another says the RSV

> *". . . followed The Eclectic Principle, which states, 'No one type of text is infallible; each reading must be examined on its own merits.' For this reason these translators did not feel bound to abiding by the most popular translations of certain passages."*[99]

In the end, the ESV and the RSV are basically from the same Greek text concocted in the nineteenth century by Westcott and Hort in their opposition to the Greek text underlying the King James Bible.

The ESV, RSV, and New Revised Standard Version (NRSV) are all related and in the same family. This is what those who publish the grandchild (NRSV) of the RSV think of the King James Bible's Greek text.

---

[95] http://baptistbulletin.org/?p=11003

[96] http://www.bible-researcher.com/esv.html

[97] http://www.bible-researcher.com/esv.html

[98] http://english.turkcebilgi.com/Revised+Standard+Version

[99] http://www.zianet.com/maxey/Ver3.htm

*"The King James Version of the New Testament was based upon a Greek text that was **marred by mistakes, containing the accumulated errors** of fourteen centuries of manuscript copying. It was essentially the Greek text of the New Testament as edited by Beza, 1598, who closely followed that published by Erasmus, 1516-1535, which was based upon a few medieval manuscripts. The earliest and best of the eight manuscripts which Erasmus consulted was from the tenth century, and he made the least use of it because it differed most from the commonly received text; Beza had access to two manuscripts of great value, dating from the fifth and sixth centuries, but he made very little use of them because they differed from the text published by Erasmus* (Emphasis added by DCB)."[100]

So what versions do the "conservative" schools promote? Well, Rodney J. Decker mentioned earlier, professor of New Testament and Greek at Baptist Bible Seminary, Clarks Summit, PA, asks:

"Is the NIV11 a viable, usable translation in Regular Baptist churches? My judgment is that the NIV11 is a usable translation in many situations, one that some of our churches will continue to use effectively."[101]

This is interesting. A professor at a Seminary approved by the GARBC before the approval system of schools was dismantled endorses the NIV11 (2011 date) while at the 2011 Southern Baptist Convention, a resolution was

"passed by convention messengers that calls the New International Version (NIV) 2011 Bible an 'inaccurate translation' the SBC cannot recommend."[102]

AND I THOUGHT THE SBC WAS LIBERAL!

What did the SBC messengers see as a problem with the NIV 2011

---

[100] http://www.ncccusa.org/newbtu/aboutrsv.html

[101] http://baptistbulletin.org/?p=18062

[102]

http://www.bpnews.net/bpnews.asp?id=35663&ref=BPNews-RSSFeed0629

version? The NIV11 (the gender-neutral edition of 2011):

> "*maintains 75 percent of the gender-neutral changes
> found in the TNIV, according to the Council on Biblical
> Manhood and Womanhood, a Louisville, Ky.-based group
> that supports a complementarian position on manhood
> and womanhood. CBMW did acknowledge that the NIV
> 2011 had 'numerous commendable improvements' from
> the TNIV but that the newest translation still had
> problems from CBMW's perspective. The NIV 2011,
> CBMW contends, changes the meaning of the text in
> numerous verses, and by changing singular pronouns to
> plural pronouns, 'removes the emphasis on an individual,
> personal relationship with God and on specific individual
> responsibility for one's choices and actions.'*"[103]

Nevertheless for professor Decker the NIV11 (dated 2011),

> "*not only communicates the meaning of God's revelation
> accurately, but does so in English that is easily
> understood by a wide range of English speakers. It is as
> well suited for expository preaching as it is for public
> reading and use in Bible classes and children's
> ministries.*"[104]

However, Decker does admit the NIV11 has some "*warts.*" One of

> "*The bigger warts in the NIV11 include Romans 16:1 and
> 2, in which Phoebe is described as a deacon—potentially
> problematic in some churches, but that depends on the
> function of deacons in a particular church.*"[105]

Pretty big wart for most Independent Baptist preachers! But with time, the preachers from these schools that have professors such as Decker will have women deacons as well.

Will the preachers coming out of Baptist Bible Seminary in Clarks Summit be discerning in this matter of the differences between the various English versions and the King James Bible? No, most of these preachers will not be

---

[103] Ibid.

[104] http://baptistbulletin.org/?p=18062

[105] Ibid.

discerning enough to simply know that IF THEY ARE DIFFERENT THEY ARE NOT THE SAME.

It is also worth mentioning that Straub says the late 19th century scholar *"John William Burgon and some of his associates argued for the KJV against the Revised Version—not because the KJV was a superior English translation but because the underlying Greek text was a better Greek text than the RV used (the Westcott and Hort text)."*[106]

This is not entirely true. Dean John William Burgon wrote that

"The English (as well as the Greek) of the newly 'Revised Version' is hopelessly at fault. It is to me simply unintelligible how a company of Scholars can have spent ten years in elaborating such a very unsatisfactory production. Their uncouth phraseology and their jerky sentences, their pedantic obscurity and their unidiomatic English, contrast painfully with 'the happy turns of expression, the music of the cadences, the felicities of the rhythm' of our Authorized Version. The transition from one to the other, as the Bishop of Lincoln remarks, is like exchanging a well-built carriage for a vehicle without springs, in which you get jolted to death on a newly-mended and rarely-traversed road. But the 'Revised Version' is inaccurate as well; exhibits defective scholarship, in countless places."[107]

One can only imagine what Dean John William Burgon would say about today's ESV and NIV11. Contrary to most Seminary professors and scholars of our day, Dean John William Burgon had high regard for the Authorized Bible and its translators. He said:

"those men understood their craft! 'There were giants in those days.' As little would they submit to be bound by the new cords of the Philistines as by their green withes. Upon occasion, they could shake themselves free from

---

[106] http://baptistbulletin.org/?p=16763

[107] John William Burgon, The Revision Revised, Conservative Classics, Paradise, Pa., p. vi.

either. And why? For the selfsame reason: viz. because the SPIRIT of their GOD was mightily upon them."[108]

REMEMBER, DEAR READER, IF THEY ARE DIFFERENT THEY ARE NOT THE SAME! STICK WITH THE KING JAMES BIBLE!

---

[108] John William Burgon, The Revision Revised, Conservative Classics, Paradise, Pa., p. 196

APPENDIX B

A COMPLETE BIBLE OR
A TENTATIVE BIBLE?

After a person comes by faith to the Lord Jesus Christ as their personal Saviour from the penalty and power of sin (Ephesians 2:8 *"For by grace are ye saved through faith..."* and Romans 10:17 *"So then faith cometh by hearing, and hearing by the word of God."*), their new life is basically wrapped up in faith; faith in God and faith in God's Words (2 Corinthians 5:7 *"(For we walk by faith, not by sight:)"* !

The believer then (or at least) should have a desire to memorize God's Words so as not to sin against Him (Psalm 119:11 *"Thy word have I hid in mine heart, that I might not sin against thee."*). They take His Word as a comfort when the world opposes them (Psalm 119:42 *"So shall I have wherewith to answer him that reproacheth me: for I trust in thy word."*) and they allow His Word to guide them as they walk in this darkened sin-cursed world (Psalm 119:105 *"Thy word is a lamp unto my feet, and a light unto my path."*)

With these things in mind, I ask, is it therefore important whether God's Words are complete and completely true or simply tentative? Most would say yes, it is very important that God's Words are complete and in that, it is also completely true. As another has written:

> *"How can we be sure that anything in the Bible is true? How can we be sure that Jesus Christ is who he said he was, or even that he existed, if the Bible is not inerrant?"*[109]

---

[109]Daniel B. Wallace, MY TAKE ON INERRANCY, August 10, 2006, p.2, www.bible.org

By inerrant is meant *"without error or mistake.*" Now this might be an appropriate time to interject that *"inerrancy*" for our English Bible does not mean that there may be no printing mistakes, but it does mean the 1611 translators have accurately translated (brought across) those words from the original inspired Words in Greek over into the English language. Therefore, I believe, a person can take by faith the absolute accuracy and truthfulness of the King James Bible. Otherwise, how could one know what place or places in the Bible can or cannot be trusted? **How could anyone rest their eternal soul upon the Words of a Bible if it is not true and accurate in its entirety?**

However, there are those who, like Satan, ask:

"Yea, hath God said. . .?"[110]

What is surprising to this writer is that those scholars who question the accuracy and authenticity of the Words of the Bible are what some even claim to be *evangelical.*[111]

Let it be known these *"scholars"* are not just questioning the accuracy and trustworthiness of the translation of the King James Bible, but the accuracy, authenticity, completeness and truthfulness of the Greek Text underlying the King James Bible; and this they question in numerous places.

One such Scripture under the cloud of suspicion for these scholars is the last twelve verses of the Gospel of Mark. For instance, this *"evangelical scholar*" Dr. Bruce Metzger has written:

> *"How did Mark end his Gospel? **Unfortunately, we do not know** (Emphasis added by DCB); the most that can be said is that four different endings are current among the manuscripts but probably none of them represents what Mark originally intended."*[112]

---

[110] Genesis 3:1

[111] Daniel B. Wallace, MY TAKE ON INERRANCY, August 10, 2006, p. 4 "Bruce Metzger is an evangelical scholar", www.bible.org

[112] Bruce Metzger, THE TEXT OF THE NEW TESTAMENT ITS TRANSMISSION, CORRUPTION, AND RESTORATION, FOURTH EDITION, OXFORD

You read it correctly! Here is a *"scholar"* who some claim to be an evangelical, writing that **we do not know the true ending of the Gospel of Mark!** In fact, he doesn't STOP there. He says there are four current endings and **NONE** of them **are probably correct! If none of the four endings are true, where is that original true ending?**

Well, do not worry, someone is out there searching for it. For instance, the sixth point under the Mission for The Center for the Study of New Testament Manuscripts is

> *"To cooperate with other institutes in the great and noble task of determining the wording of the autographa of the New Testament."*[113]

This organization is **searching for God's Words** and when they find a copy of a New Testament manuscript, they will study it in the hope of *"DETERMINING THE WORDING OF THE AUTOGRAPHA OF THE NEW TESTAMENT."* This IS one of their points for existing in 2012!

This writer is not against gathering manuscripts and studying them, but if its sole purpose is solely done to ascertain the true reading of God's Words because they believe we do not yet have a complete Bible, then I am against it. Think about it, if we do not presently, at this time in 2012, have what God has said and particularly in this case what Mark wrote, what kind of a Bible do we have? **Do we have a complete Bible, or a tentative Bible?** The answer to that is: those who are searching with the intent of hopefully someday restoring the Words of the Bible only possess at this present time a tentative Bible, whether in Greek or English.

Now, because the *"scholars"* question the authenticity of numerous Scriptures, but in particular the last twelve verses of Mark, in April of 2007, Southeastern Baptist Theological Seminary hosted a debate about this very question entitled; *"The Last 12 Verses of Mark: Original or Not?"*[114]

The participants

> *"included Dallas Theological Seminary's Darrell Bock, a New Testament professor, and Daniel Wallace, a New*

UNIVERSITY PRESS, 2005, p. 322.

[113] http://www.csntm.org/home/about

[114] http://www.bpnews.net/bpnews.asp?id=25663

*Testament and Greek professor; Keith Elliott, a professor
of New Testament at the University of Leeds in England;
and two professors of Greek and New Testament at
Southeastern, Maurice Robinson and David Alan
Black.*"[115]

The last two men defended the authenticity of Mark's gospel while Elliot and Wallace argued against its authenticity.

*"Bock responded to both views with a final presentation
on the state of current research."*[116]

For this writer it was no surprise what position Daniel Wallace would take, but sadly the Baptist Press News article did not give Bock's response and what he believed. Nevertheless, a little searching of the internet found one source who seems to have either been there or had firsthand knowledge of how Bock responded. This source has written:

*"I think Dr. Bock spent too much time refuting the longer
ending than responding to all of the presenters. I wonder
why he had nothing negative to say about Dr. Wallace's
position–a position to which he holds."*[117]

Therefore, Bock's position concerning the last twelve verses of Mark is that of Wallace's, which should come as no real surprise since he too is a Dallas Seminary professor.

From that debate, it seems to come down to basically two views which a person can take when it comes to the last twelve verses of Mark's gospel. Those **two views are that those verses are either authentic or not authentic.**

Taking that last view, that they are not authentic, it seems to be saying that, by faith, one believes that God moved certain men to write what is called Scripture (inspiration) so that those Words could and would eventually be lost. Therefore, in taking this view, the result is that there must be a continual search for those Words with the hope of someday **restoring** Scripture to the form it

---

[115] Ibid.

[116] Ibid.

[117] http://www.alanknox.net/2007/04/last-twelve-verses-of-mark-conference_5808/

took when the original authors wrote?

Or do we by faith believe that God **protected and preserved** His Words after they were written by the human authors and then copied and recopied many times over so that today, 2013, we have an accurate, authentic, complete copy of those original inspired Greek Words? Based upon that premise, those of us who hold to the superiority of the King James Bible can say we have an accurate complete English translation of those original inspired Words from a **complete** Greek Text!

But again, there may be some who ask "In the end does it really matter which view a believer makes?" Well, as Dr. Floyd Nolan Jones has written:

> *"Until the matter is settled in favor of 'preservation,' the worker will always have a 'tentative' Bible."*[118]

A *"tentative"* Bible! A tentative Bible is not a settled Bible. A tentative Bible is not a complete Bible. A tentative Bible is an uncertain Bible.

Let's take time to refresh our memory in the fact that God's Words in the New Testament was originally written in Greek. So the dispute today is not just about what English Bible one should use, it is also about the Greek Text from which that English Bible was translated.

So what Greek Text should underlie an accurate English, or any other language translation? Generally speaking, most consider there being two Greek Texts, the Textus Receptus (TR or often called the Received Text) and the Critical Greek Text birthed by Westcott and Hort.

Here we will again reiterate the question *"In the end does it really matter which view a believer makes?"* The answer is *"yes,"* it does matter. There is a great difference between the two Greek Texts. Let an advocate of the Critical Greek text answer whether there are any differences between the two or not. Daniel Wallace writes:

"the differences between the New Testament of the King James Version, for example, and that of the New American Standard Version are not just differences in the English; there are also differences in the Greek text behind the

---

[118] Floyd Nolan Jones, The Chronology of the Old Testament, Master Books, Green Forest, AR, page 10.

English—in fact, over 5,000 differences!"[119]

[Dr. Jack Moorman has written an excellent book which catalogs over **8,000 differences** between the New Testament Received Greek Text underlying the King James Bible and the Gnostic Critical Greek Text. It is **BFT #3084** @ **$20.00 + S&H.** DAW]

Note Wallace agrees **there is a difference** and that it is not just one or two or even one hundred BUT there are over **5,000 differences** in these two **Texts.** Mind you, this is someone who supports the Critical Text saying this!

In all probability, this present discussion would not be happening if it was not for those two Anglican churchmen, Westcott and Hort. As early as:

> *"At the age of 23, in late 1851, Hort wrote to a friend: 'I had no idea till the last few weeks of the importance of texts, having read so little Greek Testament, and dragged on with the villainous Textus Receptus. . . . Think of that vile Textus Receptus leaning entirely on late MSS.; it is a blessing there are such early ones.'"*[120]

Hort wrote that the Textus Receptus was both *"villainous"* and *"vile."* There was no love lost here and the outcome was the Critical Greek Text. The Textus Receptus had always had its enemies but it was the Westcott and Hort Critical Greek Text that really birthed what is seen today with the publication of a multitude of English Versions. Not only has there been a massive publishing of new English Versions but the Critical Greek Text has not been untouched either. These people are in **search of God's Words** and are hoping to someday have it in their possession, but until then, they continue to publish new versions and Greek texts.

For instance, when I was in Bible College in the early seventies, we used

---

[119] Daniel B. Wallace, Inspiration, Preservation, and New Testament Textual Criticism, Originally published in *Grace Theological Journal* 12 (1992) 21-51; also published in *New Testament Essays in Honour of Homer A. Kent, Jr.* (ed. Gary T. Meadors; Winona Lake, IN: BMH Books, 1991): 69-102.

[120] http://www.revisedstandard.net/text/WNP/id_3.html

the United Bible Societies Second Edition of The Greek New Testament. In the Preface of this edition, it said that the Committee responsible for this Text had four stages in which it carried out its work. The first stage was

"*on the basis of Westcott and Hort's edition of the Greek New Testament.*"[121]

The United Bible Societies now have a 4th Revised Edition of The Greek New Testament.[122]

In my UBS Edition, on page ix it mentions the 25th edition of the Nestle-Aland Greek Text. But since then it too has been revised and there is now a 27th edition. Will this searching of "*manuscripts in order to weigh which reading is thought closest to the original*"[123] ever cease? Probably not?

In fact Westcott and Hort's Critical Greek text became so popular with those who despised the Textus Receptus that one has said

"*For the first two-thirds of the twentieth century, NT textual critics could speak with one accord: The textus receptus (TR) had finally been laid to rest. In 1899 Marvin Vincent referred to it as an 'historical monument' that 'has been summarily rejected as a basis for a correct text.' A. T. Robertson in 1926 declared: 'The Textus Receptus is as dead as Queen Anne.' Eight years later Leo Vaganay similarly pronounced last rites over the corpse. And just three decades ago Bruce Metzger could justifiably dismiss the contemporary defense of the*

---

[121] THE GREEK NEW TESTAMENT, 2nd Edition, United Bible Societies, 1968, Preface p. v.

[122] http://www.ubs-translations.org/cat/biblical_texts/greek_scriptures_and_reference/new_testament/

[123]

http://en.wikipedia.org/wiki/Novum_Testamentum_Graece#Current_editions

Byzantine text in a mere footnote."[124]

Bruce Metzger who may have reviled the TR as much as Hort did, wrote that

> "*The year 1881 was marked by the publication of the*
> **most noteworthy** *critical edition of the Greek Testament*
> *ever produced by British scholarship. After working about*
> *28 years on this edition of Peterborough and regius*
> *professor of divinity at Cambridge (consecrated bishop of*
> *Durham in 1890), and Fenton John Anthony Hort (1828-*
> *1892), Hulsean Professor of Divinity at Cambridge,*
> *issued two volumes entitled The New Testament in the*
> *Original Greek.*"[125]

The first English Version translated from this Westcott and Hort Critical Text was the Revised Version of the New Testament. Both saw the light of day in 1881. However, take a moment and go back up to the last paragraph to observe Metzger's words "**most noteworthy.**" Bruce Metzger views this Greek Text of Westcott and Hort's that omits numerous portions of Scripture as "**most noteworthy**". Why? Because it promotes what seems to be his own view that all we can ever really possess is a tentative Bible.

Daniel Wallace bestows upon the Critical Text as the "*epoch-making publication*"[126] of Westcott and Hort. Here Wallace agrees with Metzger for he too argues that if we continue our search for manuscript evidence we can then "*. . . have **relative** certainty that we can get back to the*

---

[124] Daniel B. Wallace, The Majority Text Theory: History, Methods and Critique, *JETS* 37/2 (June 1994) p. 185.

[125] Bruce Metzger, THE TEXT OF THE NEW TESTAMENT Its Transmission, Corruption, and Restoration, FOURTH EDITION, OXFORD UNIVERSITY PRESS, 2005, p. 174

[126] Daniel B. Wallace, THE MAJORITY TEXT THEORY: HISTORY, METHODS AND CRITIQUE, JOURNAL OF THE EVANGELICAL THEOLOGICAL SOCIETY, June 1994, pp. 186, 187

wording of the autographs."[127]

Note the word "<u>relative.</u>" An antonym of **"relative"** used in conjunction with certainty is **absolute!** Will these people **EVER** have a **COMPLETE** Bible?

Westcott and Hort were the parents of this New Greek Text which has become known as the Critical Text, and in their opinion it is

"the most free from later corruption and mixture and the nearest to the text of the autographs. It is best represented by Codex Vaticanus (B) and next by Codex Sinaiticus (ℵ). The concurrence of these two manuscripts is very strong and shows that they cannot be far from the original text."[128]

In the high esteem for these two manuscripts (especially B) they wrote

"It is our belief (1) that the readings of ℵ B should be accepted as the true readings until strong internal evidence is found to the contrary, and (2) that no readings of ℵ B can safely be rejected absolutely, though it is sometimes right to place them only on an alternative footing, especially where they receive no support from Versions or Fathers."[129]

The followers of Westcott and Hort continue the adoration of these two manuscripts and especially that of Vaticanus B. For example, Bruce Metzger wrote:

"One of the most valuable of all the manuscripts of the

---

[127] http://www.csntm.org/

[128] Bruce Metzger, THE TEXT OF THE NEW TESTAMENT Its Transmission, Corruption, and Restoration, FOURTH EDITION, OXFORD UNIVERSITY PRESS, 2005, p.179

[129] Ibid.

Greek Bible is Codex Vaticanus."[130]

To be fair, Metzger did write later that

"*. . . most scholars have abandoned Hort's optimistic view that Codex Vaticanus (B) contains the original text almost unchanged except for slips of the pen, they are still inclined to regard the Alexandrian text as on the whole the best ancient recension and the one most nearly approximating the original.*"[131]

Westcott and Hort placed so much confidence in these two manuscripts, א & B that they were willing to mutilate numerous passages including the impugning and complete deletion of the last twelve verses of Mark. In defense of these last twelve verses, John Burgon (1813–1888) justly wrote:

"*The text of the sacred deposit is far too precious a thing to be sacrificed to an irrational, or at least a superstitious devotion to two MSS.,--simply because they may possibly be older by a hundred years than any other which we possess.*"[132]

YES, the Words of God is too PRECIOUS to allow what these two men did and what their followers continue to do!

In fact, in the Gospel of Mark Chapter 16, this venerated Westcott and Hort,

"*B leaves a whole blank column – 'the only blank one in the whole volume' –i.e., of the New Testament, as well as the rest of the one containing v. 8, thus showing that a*

---

[130] Ibid., p.67

[131] Ibid. p. 312

[132] Dean John Burgon, The Last Twelves verse of Mark, The Dean Burgon Society, Box 354, Collingswood, NJ 08108, p. 76

passage was left out."[133] [134]

Westcott and Hort could rightfully be called the fathers of those today who are continuing the critical search for the lost Words of God. Westcott and Hort wrote in the Introduction to their Greek New Testament that

> *"This edition is __an attempt__ to present exactly the original words of the New Testament, __so far as they can now be determined__ from surviving documents."*[135]

Note the words **"an attempt"** and **"so far as they can be determined"**. Is this **"an attempt"** simply **"a stab in the dark"**?[136] Using the words *"__An attempt__"* and *"__so far as can be determined__"* are not words that would give confidence in a Bible produced by these people!

These two, Westcott and Hort, set out to produce their own Greek Text because of what they thought they saw and believed was the

> *"unworthiness of the Received texts. . . ."*[137]

Now this Received Text that was so unworthy in the eyes of Westcott and Hort was and still is based on the **majority of manuscript evidence**. This critical view of the majority of evidence was also held by others before Westcott and Hort. In Germany, which is infamous for two world wars, its "scholars" such as Johann Jakob Griesbach (1745–1812) are infamous as well, but for their textual criticism. For example, Metzger wrote:

---

[133] Edward Miller, A Guide to the Textual Criticism of the New Testament, Dean Burgon Society Press, Box 354, Collingswood, NJ, p. 126.

134

http://images.csntm.org/Manuscripts/GA_03/GA_03_0037a.jpg
This blank column may be viewed at this site.

[135] The New Testament in the Original Greek, Introduction, p. 2

[136] "to take a complete guess"
http://www.idiomeanings.com/idioms/take-a-stab-in-the-dark/

[137] The New Testament in the Original Greek, Introduction, p.

16

"Griesbach showed great skill and tact in evaluating the evidence of variant readings. For example, his judgment, based on patristic and versional evidence, that the shorter form of the Lord's Prayer in Luke 11:3-4 is to be preferred was remarkably confirmed a few years later when the readings of Codex Vaticanus were published, for it was found that all of the omissions are supported by that early manuscript. The importance of Griesbach for New Testament textual criticism can scarcely be overestimated. For the first time in Germany a scholar ventured to abandon the Textus Receptus at many places and to print the text of the New Testament in the form to which his investigations had brought him."[138]

All this manuscript evidence was abandoned and shoved aside by Westcott and Hort as well and it continues to be abandoned and shoved aside by their followers. These followers of Griesbach, Westcott and Hort continue their critical search hoping to restore God's Word someday. Why do they abandon and thrust aside the majority of manuscript evidence? It is simply because (1) they despise the TR and (2) the majority of manuscript evidence is not dated as early as B and א. Surprisingly Westcott and Hort do admit that "A glance at any tolerably complete apparatus criticus of the Acts or Pauline Epistles reveals the striking fact that an overwhelming proportion of the variants common to the great mass of cursive and late uncial Greek MSS are identical with readings followed by Chrysostom (ob. 407) in the composition of his Homilies."[139]

---

[138] Bruce Metzger, The Text of the New Testament Its Transmission, Corruption, and Restoration, Fourth Edition, Oxford University Press, 2005, p. 167

[139] The New Testament in the Original Greek, Introduction, p. 91

They continue in confirming the early date for those manuscripts underlying the TR by writing that

> "*The fundamental text of the late extant Greek MSS generally is beyond all question identical with the dominant Antiochian or Graeco-Syrian text of the second half of the fourth century.*"[140]

So from the pen of Westcott and Hort themselves, one can go back as far as the second-half of the fourth century to find an identical text that is today known as the Received Text!

It is well known that the published text which became known as the Textus Receptus preceded the Critical Greek Text of Westcott and Hort by over three hundred years. This TR was first published by Erasmus in 1516, and according to Bruce Metzger, the printed text of Erasmus was so popular that

> "*Within 3 years a second edition was called for, and the total number of copies of the 1516 and 1519 editions amounted to 3,300. The second edition became the basis of Luther's German translation.*"[141]

People were hungry for the Words of God and what they received was the Received Text!

However, it is very important to mention here that the King James Bible is not reliant solely on any single TR text. As G. W. and D. E. Anderson write

> "*F. H. A. Scrivener (1813-1891) attempted to reproduce as exactly as possible the Greek text which underlies the Authorised Version of 1611. However, the AV was not translated from any one printed edition of the Greek text. The AV translators relied heavily upon the work of William Tyndale and other editions of the English Bible.*"

---

[140] The New Testament in the Original Greek, Introduction, p. 92

[141] Bruce Metzger, THE TEXT OF THE NEW TESTAMENT Its Transmission, Corruption, and Restoration, FOURTH EDITION, OXFORD UNIVERSITY PRESS, 2005, p.145

> *Thus there were places in which it is unclear what the Greek basis of the New Testament was. Scrivener in his reconstructed and edited text used as his starting point the Beza edition of 1598, identifying the places where the English text had different readings from the Greek. He examined eighteen editions of the Textus Receptus to find the correct Greek rendering, and made the changes to his Greek text. When he finished he had produced an edition of the Greek New Testament which more closely underlies the text of the AV than any one edition of the Textus Receptus.*"[142]

This writer has a copy of *Scrivener's Annotated Greek New Testament* printed by the Dean Burgon Society.[143] The inside cover of this Greek New Testament states that this is *"the exact Greek Textus Receptus that underlies the King James Bible."* It goes on to affirm that this Greek New Testament shows

> *"the E.R.V. 1881/Westcott and Hort Erroneous Departures from the Textus Receptus."*

It is this Greek Text that gave us English-speaking people a COMPLETE ENGLISH BIBLE!

So, in the end, it really then comes down to faith, as to whether or not God has **protected and preserved** His original inspired Words so they can be faithfully translated into other languages. As far as the Authorized Version's Greek Text, Dr. Floyd Nolan Jones believes

> *"this preserved Text has best and most faithfully been rendered into English by the AD 1611 King James*

---

[142] G. W. and D. E. Anderson, The Received Text A Brief Look at the Textus Receptus, *Quarterly Record* no. 546, January to March 1999, Trinitarian Bible Society

[143] Scrivener's Annotated Greek New Testament, Dean Burgon Society Press, Box 354, Collingswood, NJ, 08108, USA, 1999

translators."[144]

Today the Critical Greek Text folk recognize there is a movement afoot promoting the view that the King James Bible is the superior English Bible due to its underlying Greek Text. Those within this movement believe they are the preserved inspired Greek Words of God. In fact some of those within the movement have prompted Daniel Wallace to write that the days are gone when those who hold this view are supposedly only found in

"*the backwaters of anti-intellectual American fundamentalism.*"[145]

According to Wallace, this movement in defense of Burgon's view and the TR was so minuscule and ignorant that

". . . *just three decades ago Bruce Metzger could justifiably dismiss the contemporary defense of the Byzantine text in a mere footnote*"[146]

But all of that has now changed, Wallace says, for

"*in the third edition of The Text of the New Testament it was now necessary for Metzger to devote five pages to a discussion of the resuscitation of John Burgon's views.*"[147]

Wallace goes on to state that

"*Although there was a hiatus of almost seven decades between Burgon and the **next scholarly defender** of the traditional text, virtually all such defenders today rely on*

[144]Floyd Nolan Jones, The Chronology of the Old Testament, Master Books, Green Forest, AR, page 17.

[145] Daniel B. Wallace, THE MAJORITY TEXT THEORY: HISTORY, METHODS AND CRITIQUE, JOURNAL OF THE EVANGELICAL THEOLOGICAL SOCIETY, June 1994, p. 185

[146] Ibid.

[147] Ibid., p. 186

Burgon for impetus and articulation."[148]

The words to note in what Wallace has to say here are "*next scholarly defender.*" Wallace does see within this movement those who are capable students of the Greek language of the Bible.

Now this writer is not one of those which Wallace would probably consider a scholarly defender of Burgon, or the Greek Text, but he is one which has read to some extent on the subject. But beyond that reading, he has come to his position by faith that God, in His providence, gave us His preserved inspired Words in the Greek text used by our 1611 King James translators and they accurately brought over into our English language those very Words. Therefore, today, we do not have a TENTATIVE Bible but a COMPLETE Bible!

It has taken this writer longer than he intended to, but it has been referred to in various places in this paper, that Daniel Wallace, Metzger, and others like them, have been saying that the Greek Text (TR) that believers had before the 19th century, was corrupt! Metzger echoes this sentiment, when he wrote that

> "*For almost two centuries scholars ransacked libraries and museums, in Europe as well as the Near East, for weaknesses to the text of the New Testament. But almost all of the editors of the New Testament during this period were content to reprint the time-honored but corrupt Textus Receptus. . . .*"[149]

Poor souls those early believers were, in that they believed they had the Words of God in the TR, but they only had a CORRUPT Text! Or so says Metzger!

Again, calling the TR corrupt and poking his finger at Burgon, Metzger wrote that

> "*What Burgon was apparently unable to comprehend was*

---

[148] Ibid.

[149] Bruce Metzger, THE TEXT OF THE NEW TESTAMENT Its Transmission, Corruption, and Restoration, FOURTH EDITION, OXFORD UNIVERSITY PRESS, 2005, p. 153

the force of the genealogical method, by which the later,
conflated text is demonstrated to be secondary and
corrupt."[150]

Why did Burgon do this? Well, as Metzger said:

". . . *Burgon preferred the readings supported by the*
majority of the later witnesses."[151]

One will find when reading Burgon and Miller's books, that Burgon's reliance on the majority of manuscript evidence is only part of his confidence for the Greek New Testament, but he also looked to the witness of the Fathers, Lectionaries, and Versions.

Metzger adds

"*Consequently, so far from sharing Westcott and Hort's*
high regard for the testimony of Codex Vaticanus and
Codex Sinaiticus, Burgon maintained that, with the single
exception of D, which exhibits the wildest text of all, the
two manuscripts honored by Westcott and Hort are the
*most **depraved**.*"[152]

Metzger is truthful here in the fact that Burgon looked upon Westcott and Hort's venerably honored manuscripts as "**depraved**"!

This writer has never found a man with whom he has totally agreed (outside of those whom God moved to write His inspired Words) and that goes for Dean John William Burgon. While I am but a pygmy, and he a giant, there are a few areas where I would disagree. But, on the whole, I would rather side with Brother Burgon than with Westcott and Hort.

Having said that, and not desiring to wear out the reader, let us allow Brother Burgon to speak for himself concerning the work of Westcott and Hort (Emphasis added is by DCB).

"*WHATEVER may be urged in favour of Biblical*

---

[150] Ibid., 181

[151] Ibid., 182

[152] Ibid.

*Revision, it is at least undeniable that the undertaking involves a <u>tremendous risk</u>. Our Authorized Version is the one religious link which at present binds together ninety millions of English-speaking men scattered over the earth's surface. Is it reasonable that **so unutterably precious, so sacred a bond should be endangered, for the sake of representing certain words more accurately**, — here and there translating a sense with greater precision,—getting rid of a few archaisms? It may be confidently assumed that no 'Revision' of our Authorized Version, however judiciously executed, will ever occupy the place in public esteem which is actually enjoyed by **the work of the Translators of 1611, — the noblest literary work in the Anglo-Saxon language.***

*"We shall in fact never have another 'Authorized Version.' And this single consideration may be thought absolutely fatal to the project, except in a greatly modified form. To be brief,—As a companion in the study and for private edification: as a book of reference for critical purpose, especially in respect of difficult and controverted passages:—we hold that **a revised edition of the Authorized Version** of our English Bible, (if executed with consummate ability and learning,) **would at any time be a work of inestimable value.** The method of such a performance, whether by marginal Notes or in some other way, we forbear to determine. **But only as a handmaid is it to be desired.** As something intended to supersede our present English Bible, we are thoroughly convinced that the project of a rival Translation is not to be entertained for a moment. For ourselves, we deprecate it entirely.*

"On the other hand, who could have possibly foreseen what has actually come to pass since the Convocation of the Southern Province (in Feb. 1870) declared itself favourable to 'a Revision of the Authorized Version,' and appointed a Committee of Divines to undertake the work?

Who was to suppose that the Instructions given to the Revisionists would be by them systematically disregarded? __Who was to imagine that an utterly untrustworthy 'new Greek Text,' constructed on mistaken principles, — (say rather, on no principles at all,)__ —would be the __fatal result__? To speak more truly, — Who could have anticipated that the opportunity would have been adroitly seized to inflict upon the Church the text of Drs Westcott and Hort, in all its essential features, — __a text which__, as will be found elsewhere largely explained, __we hold to be the most vicious Recension of the original Greek in existence__?

"Above all,—Who was to foresee that instead of removing 'plain and clear errors' from our Version, the Revisionists,—(besides __systematically removing out of sight so many of the genuine utterances of the SPIRIT,__)—would themselves __introduce a countless number of blemishes, unknown to it before__? Lastly, how was it to have been believed that the Revisionists would show themselves industrious in __sowing__ broadcast over four continents __doubts as to the Truth of Scripture, which__ it __will never be in their power either to remove or to recall__?"[153]

Westcott and Hort were not working with just any book, but as Burgon states:

". . . what makes this so very serious a matter is that, because HOLY SCRIPTURE is the Book experimented upon, the loftiest interests that can be named become imperilled; and it will constantly happen that what is not perhaps in itself a very serious mistake may yet inflict irreparable injury."[154]

Dean Burgon continued:

"They had a noble Version before them, which they have

[153] John Burgon, The Revision Revised, Conservative Classics, Box 308, Paradise, Pa., pp. 114, 115

[154] Ibid., p. 197

contrived to spoil in every part. Its dignified simplicity and essential faithfulness, its manly grace and its delightful rhythm, they have shown themselves alike unable to imitate and unwilling to retain. Their queer uncouth phraseology and their jerky sentences:—their pedantic obscurity and their stiff, constrained manner:—their fidgety affectation of accuracy,—and their habitual achievement of English which fails to exhibit the spirit of the original Greek;—are sorry substitutes for the living freshness, and elastic freedom, and habitual fidelity of the grand old Version which we inherited from our Fathers, and which has sustained the spiritual life of the Church of England, and of all English-speaking Christians, for 350 years. Linked with all our holiest, happiest memories, and bound up with all our purest aspirations: part and parcel of whatever there is of good about us: fraught with men's hopes of a blessed Eternity and many a bright vision of the never-ending Life; — the Authorized Version, wherever it was possible, should have been jealously retained."[155]

Allow me to offer a (few) more words of John Burgon. Speaking of Westcott and Hort, he writes:

"As Critics they have had abundant warning. Twelve years ago (1871) a volume appeared on the 'last Twelve Verses of the Gospel according to S. Mark,'—of which the declared object was to vindicate those Verses against certain critical objectors, and to establish them by an exhaustive argumentative process. Up to this hour, for a very obvious reason, no answer to that volume has been attempted. And yet, at the end of ten years (1881),—not only in the Revised English but also in the volume which professes to exhibit the underlying Greek, (which at least is indefensible,)—the Revisers are observed to separate

[155] Ibid., pp. 225, 226

off those Twelve precious Verses from their context, in token that they are no part of the genuine Gospel. Such a deliberate preference of "mumpsimus" to "sumpsimus" is by no means calculated to conciliate favour, or even to win respect. The Revisers have in fact been the dupes of an ingenious Theorist, concerning whose extraordinary views you are invited to read what Dr. Scrivener has recently put forth. The words of the last-named writer (who is facile princeps in Textual Criticism) will be found facing the beginning of the present Dedication."[156]

I am thankful that Brother Burgon enlightened us on this important matter of the New Testament Text, and the treasonous way in which the New Greek Text was birthed and promoted to the world, but *"mumpsimus"* and *"sumpsimus"*? Those words must have been missed in my first reading, so let's take a brief moment and see what *"sumpsimus"* means first.

"sump·si·mus [suhmp-*suh-muhs*]

noun, plural -mus·es for 2.

1. *adherence to or persistence in using a strictly correct term, holding to a precise practice, etc., as a rejection of an erroneous but more common form (opposed to mumpsimus).*

2. *a person who is obstinate or zealous about such strict correctness (opposed to mumpsimus).*"[157]

As for "mumpsimus";

"mump·si·mus [muhmp-*suh-muhs*]

noun, plural -mus·es for 2.

1. *adherence to or persistence in an erroneous use of language, memorization, practice, belief, etc., out of habit or obstinacy (opposed to sumpsimus).*

2. *a person who persists in a mistaken expression or practice (opposed to*

---

[156] Ibid. p. vii

[157] http://dictionary.reference.com/browse/sumpsimus

sumpsimus)."[158]

The origin of the word *"mumpsimus"* is said to come

"from a story, which perhaps originated with Erasmus, of an illiterate priest who said mumpsimus rather than sūmpsimus (1st plural perfect indicative of Latin sūmere to pick up; see <u>consume</u>) while reciting the liturgy, and refused to change the word when corrected."[159]

Perhaps something was learned here with these two words, but as to whether it will be remembered, is another story.

Hurrying on to a conclusion, when Westcott and Hort felt confident that the time was ripe, they published their New Greek Testament and in the same year the English Revised Standard Version was published as well. From then on, there was no stopping the floodgate!

So, it is safe to say, that those who hold to the Westcott and Hort theory continue to critically search for the Bible. But, those who hold to the Greek Text underlying the King James Bible, believe we possess already God's original inspired, preserved Hebrew, Aramaic, and Greek Words. And we also believe that those Words were accurately brought over, and translated into our King James Bible in 1611.

In summation, the Westcott and Hort followers believe **MAN** will someday **RESTORE** God's Words! Reiterating, but hopefully not laboriously, those holding to the underlying Greek Text of the King James Bible, believe, by faith and the manuscript evidence, that God INSPIRED, PROTECTED AND PRESERVED His Words in the Hebrew, Aramaic, and Greek Words used by our 1611 translators.

Therefore Critical Text folk will always have <u>TENTATIVE</u> Bibles whereas those who hold to the Greek Text underlying the King James Bible HAVE now and will always have a <u>COMPLETE</u> BIBLE both in Greek and English! Yes, *"The LORD hath done great things for us; whereof we are glad"*

---

[158] Ibid.

[159] Ibid.

(Psalm 126:3). We do not need to conduct expensive and time-consuming searches for manuscripts all over the world as Dan Wallace from Dallas Seminary has been doing for many years. God has preserved for us the original Hebrew, Aramaic, and Greek Words that underlie the King James Bible. Our Bible is not "**TENTATIVE**," but "**COMPLETE**."

Index of Words and Phrases

Dr. David C. Bennett

- **The Title.** This book's title is *God's Marvelous Book—The Bible*. The book not only defends the King James Bible as an excellent translation, but it also defends the Hebrew, Aramaic, and Greek Words on which the King James Bible is based.

- **The Author.** The author of this book, Dr. David Bennett, has been one of the missionaries of the 𝕭𝖎𝖇𝖑𝖊 𝕱𝖔𝖗 𝕿𝖔𝖉𝖆𝖞 𝕭𝖆𝖕𝖙𝖎𝖘𝖙 𝕮𝖍𝖚𝖗𝖈𝖍 for many years. Our church is his "sending church." He and his wife, Pam, have been serving the Lord Jesus Christ in the land of Australia. He has a church as well as a radio ministry there. He is one of our faithful Executive Committee members of the Dean Burgon Society (DBS).

- **The Purpose.** Throughout this book, Dr. Bennett has attempted to show that we have a completed Bible based on completed Hebrew, Aramaic, and Greek manuscripts. There is no need, as many are doing today, to continue to seek the proper Hebrew, Aramaic, and Greek Words. These preserved Words underlie the King James Bible. See why this is true.

www.BibleForToday.org

BFT 4050 BK   **ISBN #978-1-56848-083-1**

www.ingramcontent.com/pod-product-compliance
Lightning Source LLC
Chambersburg PA
CBHW062000040426
42447CB00010B/1837